The Art of Sewing®

A Custom Fit

A Workbook

Shirley L. Smith

The Sewing Arts®, Inc.

D1088663

Front cover: Photo by Edward Jennings

Back cover: Photo by Shirley Smith

The Sewing Arts® Inc.
 A teaching studio
For the love of sewing

First Printing: February 2000

A Sewing Arts® Book
Sewing Arts® and Art of Sewing® is a trademark of the Sewing Arts Inc

The Sewing Arts®, 175 Palos Verdes,
White Salmon, WA 98672

Library of Congress

ISBN:09621123-4-8

ACKNOWLEDGEMENTS

A book of this kind cannot be written without a great deal of experience in fitting every type of body. I am very grateful to all my private fitting clients and students for the past thirty years who presented me with the challenge of helping them to make clothing that fit, especially those ladies who came to me with special needs because of major figure variations due to curvature of the spine, hip replacements, and osteoporosis. I felt very privileged to have the knowledge to help them achieve a fit that was most comfortable and presented a measure of style.

Elizabeth Nash

I will always be grateful to her for generously sharing her knowledge of fitting, pattern drafting, couture sewing and tailoring.
Elizabeth was apprenticed to the sewing industry in Europe when she was eleven years old. She went on to become a Head Master Tailor in a couture house in Vienna, Austria. After the war, she immigrated to the United States, settling in Portland, Oregon, where I studied with her and soon learned to appreciate what a wealth of knowledge she possessed and was willing to share with me.

She taught me that the fitting process is always the first step in constructing a quality garment to achieve a custom fit. Although she had been trained in the European approach to drafting a pattern for each garment, she was quick to realize the advantages of having a wide variety of fashion patterns to choose from in the United States, and that by utilizing these patterns, the choices were virtually unlimited and the tedious European methods could be greatly enhanced. She was also quick to realize that the commercial United States fashion patterns would have to be customized to account for the fact that no two people were built exactly alike. Her solution was to take critical body measurements, apply those measurements to the commercial pattern, alter the pattern accordingly, and construct a fitting garment that was individually customized.. Elizabeth used dress forms for draping and to check design details but believed the home seamstress could more easily and accurately judge the wearing ease in fitting the dress on her own body. She believed that fashion clothing should be fitted on a moving body to judge both the wearing and design ease.

Vogue Patterns, Butterick Co.

A special Thank You to Janet DuBane of Vogue Patterns, and the Butterick Co. for allowing me to use their products in illustrating my workbook.

Judith Rasband

I am indebted to Judith Rasband for perfecting the seam method of adjusting patterns. I had used patterns at the seam lines for some easy adjustments for years but she perfected the seam method and I now use it for all adjustments. It works for difficult adjustments as well as simple ones. Her seam method has made pattern alterations much easier for everyone to understand.

A special thanks to **Linda Steider**, my model, who patiently let me photograph her through all the steps of achieving a custom fit.

And last, but not least, my thanks to my husband, Don, whose patience, interest and indispensable critical proof reading, have made this book a reality.

Dedication Page

This book is dedicated to discriminating sewers everywhere who have struggled with the problem of achieving a good fit.

To my parents: The Bromileys

My mother Lois nurtured my love of sewing through my growing up years.
My father Frank taught me by example the wisdom of perseverance and hard work.

CONTENTS

INTRODUCTION

Why write a book on fitting? Fitting is the subject which seems foremost on the minds of all sewers, from the beginner to the accomplished seamstress. Everywhere I go, whether it is in my classroom or teaching seminars in different parts of the country, the question of fit is most often voiced as the problem needing the most attention.

Although I have sewed all my life, achieving a proper fit was always the challenge until, first I had the opportunity to study under the late Elizabeth Nash, where I learned the basics of body measurements and pattern adjustments, and then to teach in my workshop studio where I was challenged by fitting so many different figures.

While I studied every method of pattern fitting I could find, in practice, I found the method I had learned from Mrs. Nash in Portland, Oregon was the answer. That method involves taking accurate measurements, adjusting a commercial fashion pattern, making a basic fitting garment, and using the basic garment to adjust all other commercial patterns.

One thing I should make very clear from the beginning; there are no shortcuts or quick and easy methods, or "one size fits all" to creating a well-fitted garment. Doing it right requires dedication, time, and a desire to create. However, I'm sure you will find that it provides the satisfaction of knowing you have created a great fitting garment, that it is indeed a fulfilling effort, and, with some practice and experience, you will become, as I have, proficient in the application of these methods.

The first part of my workbook covers the taking of accurate measurements and leads you through adjusting a dress and pant pattern, tissue fitting the pattern, sewing the resulting dress and pant basic fitting garment, and the final step of pin fitting the garment to make any corrections or changes.

In part two of the workbook, I cover using the knowledge gained from your basic fitting garment to adjust all other commercial patterns as your very personal figure differs from the commercial patterns "average figure."

Elizabeth Nash did a dress fitting for me in 1970. I have difficult shoulders and commercial patterns were lacking in direction in correcting the problem. Using the fitting dress constructed from Mrs. Nash's pattern alterations, I could finally make comfortable clothing. Those adjustments worked for 24 years. In those 24 years, the pattern industry changed the standard dress, the years caught up with my figure, and in 1994 I again had my measurements taken, adjusted and pin fit a new tissue. I made the muslin fitting dress, pin fit it, and now use it as a basic for my new garments. The new fitting dress hangs in my closet with the date and my weight noted. My weight can vary 10 pounds with the ease I allowed in the waistband and hip line. In my particular case, my fitting garment helps keep me aware of my body shape, which in turn helps keep me weight conscious and healthy.

On a personal note, I was delighted to be pictured in a Threads Magazine article on "Fitting the Over 55 Figure." (May, 1999, Number 82.) When Senior Editor David Coffin approached me he said, "We almost didn't ask you because you don't look as if you have any figure problems." What a compliment! Truth be known, I certainly have my share of figure problems, but when clothing fits properly, it is not only comfortable, but you look great in your clothing.

I follow each of the steps set forth in this workbook when sewing for myself, for my student's garments, and for the custom fitting I do for others. Those steps produce great results. When I sew for myself, I will settle for nothing less than a well-fitted garment. I am sure everyone who sews has the very same expectations. By following the methods set forth herein, you too can make beautiful clothing THAT WILL FIT.

Denver Sewing Arts Students

Bertha's Chanel suit of Douglas Ram Samuj's hand printed fabric (imported cotton)

Dorrie's suit (quilted jacket) of Douglas Ram Samuj's hand painted fabric

Elaine's evening dress of Douglas Ram Samuj's silk chiffon

PART 1

THE BASICS OF CUSTOM FITTING

PREFACE

Industry Standard and Your Body

The fashion pattern industry standard for "A Misses" size is based on a well-proportioned and developed figure, about 5'5" tall, who wears a "B" cup bra. Dimensions are set forth on the pattern accordingly.

However, most women simply don't fit the basic profile. Rare is the lady, even one with a great figure, who is an average size according to the fashion pattern industry standard. Who among us is average? Nearly everyone must make some changes to commercial patterns to achieve a custom fit.

The steps set forth in this workbook involve taking basic body measurements, adjusting and pin fitting the pattern to reflect those measurements, sewing a basic fitting garment, and using the fitting garment to adjust commercial patterns to reflect the individual body differences from the commercial pattern industry standard.

Since virtually all American pattern companies, Vogue, Butterick, McCalls, and Simplicity's fitting garments are virtually the same your basic fitting garment and the dimensions used in constructing that garment can be used to adjust patterns from the different companies. f you use European patterns, Burda, Neu Mode, New Look or Style patterns you have a standard that fits your body to guide you in adjusting those commercial patterns.

The basic fitting muslin is used not only to adjust a commercial pattern to the differences dictated by your figure to achieve a great fit, it allows you to test the fit periodically. If you gain or lose weight or have other changes in your body shape, they are immediately apparent and the fitting muslin and your basic pattern can be adjusted to accommodate those changes.

The tissue of the basic fitting muslin can be copied, stripped of all seam allowances, hems, and used to draft custom patterns. This stripped pattern is called a sloper. Occasionally I do use the basic dress tissue as a sloper and draft patterns from it but for most of my garments, I adjust a commercial pattern. Drafting patterns is time consuming, requires special skills and most often requires a trial garment to check the fit of the drafted pattern.

Many people question me about dress forms. Dress forms have been used by the couture industry for decades, and in their very skilled hands have been used to drape fabric, perfect design ideas and be a substitute body for their clients between fittings. With the evolution of the commercial pattern, the use of dress forms by the home seamstress is being replaced by the fitting method as described in this workbook. A dress form is still valuable for draping fabric for design ideas and to perfect design details.

Adapting a commercial pattern as described in this workbook requires no special skills beyond basic sewing knowledge and carefully following the directions and produces great results.

The fitting sequence in pictures beginning with the Vogue Fitting Dress

Fashion pattern

Shirley in her fashion pattern tissue

Shirley in her basic fitting muslin

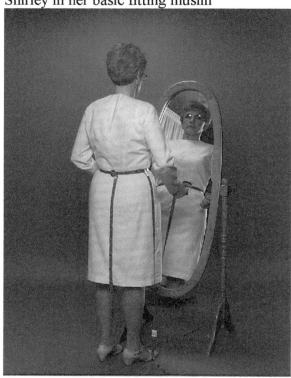

Shirley in her dress and jacket that FIT!

Chapter 1

Taking Accurate Dress Measurements

Accurate measurements are the foundation of attaining a perfect fit. Take measurements over the undergarments (bra, support garment, panty hose, or panties, and if desired a slip) that you wear with most clothing. **Measurements are without ease! (No finger under the tape).**
Equipment Needed:

- Dress Measurement Chart in this workbook on page 17 and 18.
- An eyebrow pencil for marking on the body.
- A Plumb line Kit which includes a plumb line belt and weighted drapery cord. By the Sewing Arts®, Inc.
- **Someone to take the measurements:** You cannot take your own measurements. You cannot pin fit your own muslin. If you do not have a sewing friend to assist you, hire a dressmaker to do the fitting for you. Make sure your helper gets all the information for you and takes accurate measurements.

Once your basic dress is completed you can adjust fashion patterns for yourself using the knowledge gained from the basic fitting dress and this workbook. Locating body landmarks are essential when taking accurate measurements. Those landmarks are:

Neckline: The center of the hollow at your neckline is center front neckline. The prominent bone at the base of the neck is center back neckline.

Shoulder: The shoulder pivot point is located by moving the arm up and down to feel the joint. A slight indent can often be seen. The end of the shoulder can vary but usually a hand held firmly against the upper arm reveals the location of the shoulder. A weighted string can locate a pleasing armhole (Pic 9-1).

The shoulder seam must lie exactly on the top of the profile of the shoulder (Pic 8-1).

Width: The front & back width is measured from the spot where the arm connects to the body at the high bust (Pic 8-1).

Waistline: Bend from side to side and make sure the plumb line belt is at your waist (Pic 13-1 & 22-1).

Spine: The spine at the waistline is center back. The tummy button at the waistline is center front.

Prepare for the measurements:
Place the belt (from the plumb line kit) snugly around the body just under the arms and over the chest (pic 1-1). Place a piece of cord (weighted drapery cord) from the plumb line kit around the neckline to mark a jewel neckline (pic 1-1). The weighted cord should rest at the hollow of the throat and lie on the prominent bone at the base of the neck. It must be where you are comfortable with a close fitting neckline. Join the cord ends with a couple of hand stitches.

Bodice Widths

1. High bust.

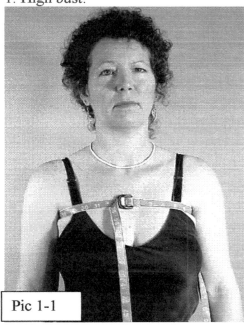

Pic 1-1

With plumb line belt or a tape level on the body, measure under the arms and over the chest.

Breathe normally. Measure with the belt. (Pic 2-1).

Pic 2-1

2. Full Bust:

Measure over the bust tip with the measuring tape level around the body, your hand holding the tape should be between the breasts (pic 3-1).

Pic 3-1

Be sure the tape measure is level around the body. Check on the profile (pic 4-1).

2a. Measure under the bust. **2b**. Note the bra and bra cup size.

Pic 4-1

3. Bust Tip Width:

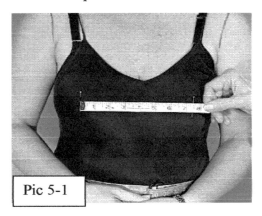

Pic 5-1

Measure from bust tip to bust tip (pic 5-1) and divide the distance in half. Leave the plumb line belt on the high bust (Pic 3-1) to measure 4, & 4a, 6 & 6a, 7, 7a & 7b. Measure to the top of the plumb line belt.

4.Front width

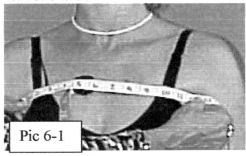

Pic 6-1

Measure across chest from the creases where the arm attaches to the body.

Divide the total front width in half since you will adjust only half of the pattern.

4a Depth of front width

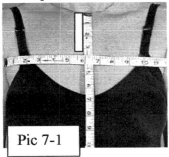

Pic 7-1

Measure the depth of the front width at center front. Measure from the top of the plumb line belt *(or in the sketch for illustrations purposes from the top of the crosswise tape)* to the jewel neckline marked by a bar (pic 7-1).

Shoulder Width and Armhole
These measurements are important for good fit and comfort in the shoulder area so take extra care and mark these landmarks on both left and right side of the body in the following manner:

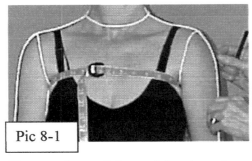

Pic 8-1

Place a piece of the weighted cord on the **profile** of the shoulder. The cord must lie exactly on top of the shoulder and should hang plumb over the shoulder and intersect the neckline cord (pic 8-1). Check the shoulder placement by moving the arm up and down to feel the shoulder joint.

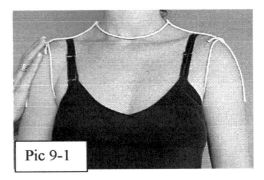

Pic 9-1

Place your hand on the upper arm to establish the position of the end of the shoulder (pic 9-1).
Place a piece of weighted cord comfortably under the arm (about ½ inch below the armhole) and lap the ends at the shoulder. Join the cord ends with a couple of hand stitches. The cord should rest at the natural armhole/shoulder junction. Make sure the weighted cords are lying exactly at the top of the shoulder (pic 8-1).

Mark the point where the cords overlap so you can measure the length of the armhole and neckline when the cord is removed.
Also mark on the cord the crease (marked on pic 10-1 with a bar) where the arm attaches to the body at the front and back armhole. This will give you the front and back depth of the armhole.

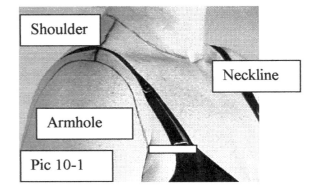

Shoulder

Neckline

Armhole

Pic 10-1

Using the eyebrow pencil, mark the position of the cords on the body at the neckline, shoulder, and armhole.

The front and back armhole depth can be measured on the body as well as on the cord by measuring along the grease pencil lines from the shoulder to the front and back creases (marked on pic 10-1 with a bar).

5. Shoulder width: Measure the pencil line at the top of the shoulder from the jewel neckline to the armhole junction. Measure the right and left shoulder (pic 10-1).

6. Back Width:

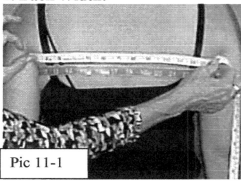

Pic 11-1

Measure across the back from the creases where the arm attaches to the body. Go slightly into the armhole creases on both sides (pic 11-1). Move the arms forward and see how much this changes. This measurement helps to determine how much ease is needed for reach room in a garment. Divide the total in half since you will adjust only half of the pattern.

6a. Depth of Back Width.

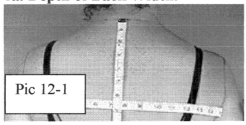

Pic 12-1

Measure from the top of the tape or belt to center back neckline, which is the prominent bone at the back of the neck (pic 12-1).

7. Armhole: Measure the armhole cord when it is removed from the body. Record the total armhole and the front and back armhole to the creases.

> **7a.** The front armhole from the shoulder to the front crease.

> **7b.** The back armhole from the shoulder to the back crease.

> These measurements are essential in judging armhole depths and widths.

8. Neckline: Measure the weighted drapery string (Pic 8-1) by marking the location of the pin or stitch holding the string around neck on either end.

Mark the location of the right and left shoulder line on the cord.

Measure the cord when it is removed from the body to determine **8a and 8b.** Measure the weighted cord when it is removed from the neckline to find the length of the front and back jewel neckline. Divide in half so that you have half the neckline.

Bodice Lengths: (shown in pic 13-1)
The body lengths that are measured from the center back at the spine bone, accurately locate the bust line, the length of the bodice front and are helpful when judging the length of skirts, shorts and one piece dresses and robes.

9. Front length to bust dart: Slip the one-inch end of the tape under the plumb line belt and measure from the center back neckline to the bust tip (pic13-1).

9a: Front length to waistline: Measure from center back over a bust tip to just under the belt directly below the bust line (pic13-1).

9b: Blouse length: Measure from center back over the bust tip to seven inches below the bottom of the belt.
This is a nice length for a blouse, which would be tucked into a skirt (pic 13-1).

9c: Bermuda length: With the one-inch mark still at the center back neckline, note a nice place on the leg above the knee for Bermuda shorts or short skirt (pic 13-1).

9d: Knee length: With the one-inch mark still at the center back neckline measure just under the kneecap. The distance from the waistline to the kneecap gives the length of a short skirt (pic 13-1).

9e: Long length: With the one-inch mark still at the center back neckline measure a long length (between the ankle and the calf of the leg) that is flattering for a skirt, dress, or coat (pic 13-1).

9f: Floor length: With the one-inch mark still at the center back neckline measure to the floor.

On any pattern with a fitted neckline you can use these measurements to check the desired length of skirts, slacks and robes (pic 13-1). **Subtract the bodice length from the total length to find the skirt or slack length**.
Bodice Lengths

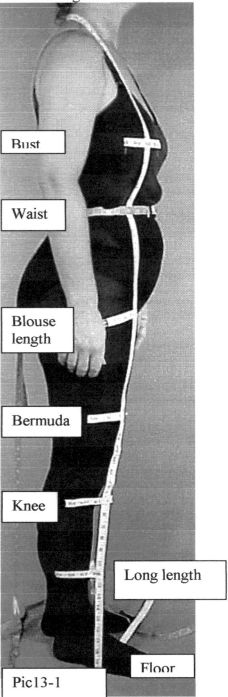

Bust

Waist

Blouse length

Bermuda

Knee

Long length

Floor

Pic13-1

Center front bodice length

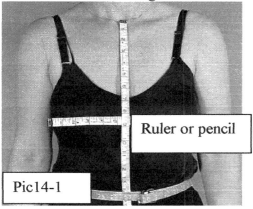

Ruler or pencil

Pic14-1

10. Center front bodice length:
Place a ruler or a pencil *(for photography a section of a stiffened tape measure was used)* across the bust line to hold the tape out the same distance as the bust and measure from the center front of the jewel neckline to the bottom of the belt (pic 14-1).

Center back bodice length

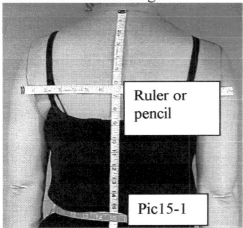

Ruler or pencil

Pic15-1

11. **Center back bodice length:** Place a ruler or a pencil *(for photography a section of a stiffened tape measure was used)* across the shoulder blades to hold the tape out the same distance as the shoulder blades and measure from the center back of the jewel neckline to the bottom of the belt (pic 15-1).

Side seam length

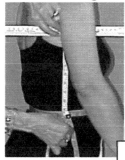

12. Side Seam Length: Place a ruler under the arm and measure from the top of the ruler to just under the belt at the side seam (pic 16-1).

Pic 16-1

This is never a very accurate measurement because of the armhole but it is helpful in judging bodice length. Bodice length is accurately adjusted at the tissue and muslin pin fit.

Shoulder Slopes

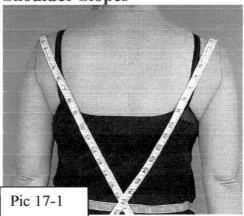

Pic 17-1

Diagonal measurements help judge the front and back length of bodice and point out asymmetrical shoulders, one larger shoulder or bust.

13. Front slope: Measure from the shoulder junction to the center front at the bottom of the belt at the waistline. (To determine center front at waistline locate the tummy button.) Measure both sides (pic17-1).

14. Back slope: Measure from the shoulder junction to the center back at the bottom of the belt at the waistline (pic17-1). (The spine is the location of the center back at waistline.) Measure both sides.

Arm Lengths

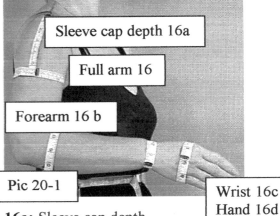

A section of a tape measure is scotch taped to mark the elbow

Pic 18-1

15. Outside arm length: With the hand in the hollow of the hip so the arm is slightly bent, measure from the shoulder junction to just below the wrist bone (pic 18-1).

15a: Measure from the shoulder to the elbow (pic 18-1).

15b: Measure from the elbow to just below the wrist bone (pic 18-1).

Arm Widths
16. Full Arm:

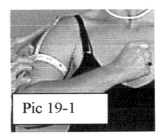

Pic 19-1

Make a fist and hold the arm against the body. Measure the fullest part of the arm at the bicep (pic 19-1).

Sleeve cap depth 16a

Full arm 16

Forearm 16 b

Pic 20-1

Wrist 16c
Hand 16d

16a: Sleeve cap depth Measure the distance from the fullest point at the biceps to the shoulder line (pic 20-1).

16b: With the fist clenched measure around the forearm just below the elbow (pic 20-1).

16c: Measure around the wrist (pic 20-1). A buttoned cuff should be about 2 inches larger than the wrist measurement.

16d: Measure around the hand with the fingers out straight and the thumb tucked in (pic 20-1). (The hand should slip easily through the circle). A closely fitted sleeve must be at least your hand measurement unless it has an opening or zipper . A buttoned cuff that your hand would slip easily through should be about 2 inches larger than the hand measurement.

Skirt Measurements

Place the plumb line belt on the waist. To determine the waist location bend from side to side to make sure the belt is at your waist. The belt should be comfortable and feel as if it is at the waistline.

Waist Line Adjustments

These measurements (pic 21-1) indicate several figure irregularities that must be adjusted at the waistline such as high or large hip, sway back and a prominent tummy or derriere. They guide the pattern adjustment at the waistline. The person being measured should hold perfectly still.

17. Waistline adjustments: Slip the

one-inch end of the tape under the belt. Bring it to the floor. Hold the 1-inch end on the floor and note the **measurement** on the tape at the bottom of the belt.

Pic 21-1

Measure at:
Center front   **Center back**
Left side   **Right side**.
Move around the person being measured.

Skirt Widths

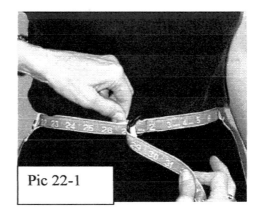

Pic 22-1

18. Waist: The plumb line belt can be used to measure the waist. Measurement should be snug but not tight (pic 22-1).

Hip Measurement

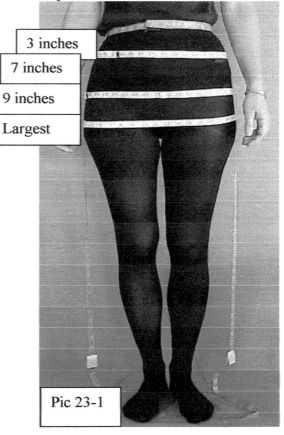

3 inches

7 inches

9 inches

Largest

Pic 23-1

The plumb line belt is used to keep the tape measure level on the body while the 3, 7, and 9-inch hip line are being measured. Picture 23-1 shows all the tapes on the hip for ease of photography.

19. Hip 3 inches from the waist: Measure with the tape even around the body (pic 23-1). This is usually the fullest part of the high hip. If the fullest part is lower, measure that and note that it is lower than 3 inches.

20. Hip 7 inches from the waist: Measure with the tape even around the body (pic 23-1).

21. Hip 9 inches from the waist: Measure with the tape even around the body (pic 23-1).

21a. Hip at the largest: Measure the largest part of the hip. The largest hip can be anywhere along the side seam. Measure the distance from the waistline to the largest part of the hip.

Tip: *The point where the plumb line belt hangs free of the hip is the largest part (pic 23-1).*

21b: The hip with the minimum wearing ease. Hold the tape between the thumb and the fingers and loosen the tape until the tape slips easily over the fullest part of the hip (pic 24-1).

Adjust the basic pattern in the correct size using the measurements plus the wearing ease allowed on the Dress Measurement Chart.

To choose your pattern size, compare your measurement in the high bust, the shoulder and the front width to the dress sizes in the Industry Standard Dress Tissue Measurement Chart.

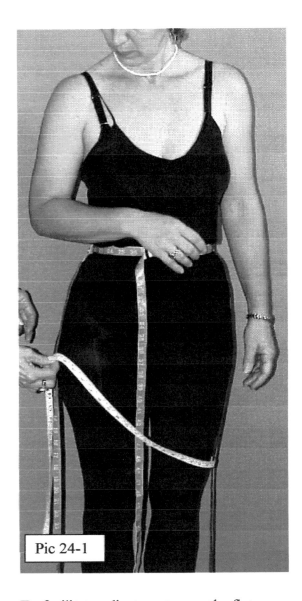

Pic 24-1

To facilitate adjustment copy the flat tissue measurements in your size to your dress measurement chart in the spaces provided.

It may be helpful to refer to Example 2: Linda's Basic Pattern and Fashion Pattern on pages 52 though57.

DRESS MEASUREMENT CHART

Personal Body Measurements: Name: _____ Date: _____

Pattern size: _____ Weight: _____

Flat Pattern Measurements from chart	**BODICE MEASUREMENTS** **BODICE WIDTHS**
1. _____	**1.** High Bust _____
2. _____	**2.** Full Bust _____ Plus 2-3 inches ease _____ **2a.**Under Bust _____
	2b. Bra size _____ cup
3. _____	**3.** Bust Tip Width_____1/2 of total width = bust dart placement on tissue _____
4. _____	**4.** Front Width____ 1/2 of total width =____ + ¼ inch ease =__
	4a Distance from center front neckline to the front width _____
5. _____	**5.**Shoulder width (front) R -____ L _____ plus 1/8-1/4inch equals Back shoulder width_____
6. _____	**6.** Back width _____1/2 of total width =_____ + 3/8 inch ease _____
	6**a.** Distance from center back neckline to the back width_____
7. _____	**7.** Armhole (measure with a weighted string. Mark shoulder & front and back arm/body crease) _____
7a. _____	**7a.** Front armhole to arm/body crease_____
7b. _____	**7b.** Back armhole to arm/body crease_____
7c.F___ B__	**7c.**_____ measure the weighted string from front armhole to back armhole
8. _____	**8.** Neckline _____(measure with weighted string & mark shoulder placement)
8a. _____	**8a**. Front neckline (½ of neckline) _____
8b. _____	**8b.** Back neckline (½ of neckline) _____
9. _____	**BODICE LENGTHS** **9.** Bust line (center back to bust tip) _____
9a. _____	**9a**. Waistline (center back over the bust tip to the waistline) _____ and on to b, c, d, e &, f
	9b. Blouse length _____**9c.** Bermuda length _____ **9d.** Knee length _____
	9e Long length _____ **9f**.Floor length _____

Flattering Lengths On Fashion Garments:
Subtract the waistline length 9a from 9c, 9d, 9e, & 9f

Bermuda length _____Knee length _____

Long length _____ Floor length _____

10. _____   **10.**Center front bodice length _____

11. _____   **11.**Center back bodice length _____

12.   **12.**Side seam length _____

SHOULDER SLOPE

13. _____   **13.** Front slope R_____ L_____

14. _____   **14.** Back slope R_____ L_____

ARM LENGTHS

15. _____   **15.** Shoulder to elbow _____

15a. _____   **15a.** Outside arm length _____

15b. _____   **15b.** Elbow to wrist _____

ARM WIDTHS

16. _____   **16.** Fullest arm (bicep) _____ + 1 ½ inches _____

16a. _____   **16a.** Shoulder to fullest arm _____

16b. _____   **16b.** Forearm. _____ **16c.**Wrist _____ **16d.** Hand _____

SKIRT MEASUREMENTS

17.   **17. Waistline Adjustments** Length From Waist To Floor
Center back _____ Left side _____

Center front _____ Right side _____

SKIRT WIDTHS
Waist & Hip Measurements⊗   (Take with a plumb line belt)

18. _____   **18.** Waist _____ +1-1 ½ inch ease _____ = waistband length _____width_____

18a._____   **18a.**Waist seam _____ ½ of waist seam _____

19. _____   **19.** 3 inches from waist _____ + 1-1 ¼ inches ease _____

20. _____   **20.** 7 inches from waist _____ + 1 3/4- 2 inches ease _____

21. _____   **21.** 9 inches from waist _____ + 2-3 inches ease _____

21a. Hip at the largest _____ Distance from waistline _____inches

21b. Tape just slips off hip line- shows minimum amount of ease
     in a close fitted skirt_____

Industry Standard Dress Tissue Measurement Chart

	VOGUE 1004						
	Size	**6**	**8**	**10**	**12**		
BODICE	**1. High bust or chest**	30 1/2	31 1/2	32 1/2	34		
WIDTHS	**2. Bust (full)**	33 3/8	34 1/4	35 3/4	37		
	1/2 bust measure	16 5/8	17 1/8	17 7/8	18 1/2		
	front tissue	8 3/4 plus	9 plus	9 3/8	9 5/8		
	back tissue	7 7/8 plus	8 1/8	8 1/2	8 3/4		
	3. Bust Tip Width	3 1/4	3 3/8	3 1/2	3 5/8		
	4. Front Width at notch	6 3/4	6 7/8	7	7 1/4		
	5. Shoulder width	4 1/2	4 3/8	4 3/4	5		
	6. Back width at notch	7 3/8	7 1/2	7 5/8	8		
7. Total armhole	7 a & b. Total front & back armhole / underarm from dot at front & back width						
	7. Armhole	14 7/8	15 7/8	16 plus	16 5/8		
	7a. Front armhole/underarm	7.5 /2 1/4	7 3/4 / 2 3/8	8 / 2 3/8	8 1/4 / 2 5/8		
	7b. Back armhole/underarm	7 3/8 /1 5/8	7 5/8 / 1 7/8	8 plus/ 2	8 3/8 / 2 1/8		
	8. Neckline	13 1/2	14	14 1/2	4 3/4 plus		
	8a. front neckline	4	4 1/8	4 1/4	4 3/8		
	8b. back neckline	2 3/4	2 7/8	2 7/8 plus	3 1/16		
BODICE	9. & 9a measurements are from center back neckline to bust symbol						
LENGTHS	**9. Center back to bust line**	12 5/8	13	13 1/4	13 3/4		
	9a. Center back to waistline	19 1/8	19 7/8	20 1/8	21 5/8		
	10. Center front bodice	14	14 1/8	14 3/8	14 3/4		
	11. Center back bodice	15 5/8	15 7/8	16 1/4	16 1/2		
	12. Side Seam	7 7/8	7 7/8	7 7/8	7 7/8		
SHOULDER	**13. Front Slope**	16 1/2	16 5/8	17	17 1/4		
SLOPE	**14. Back Slope**	16 plus	16 1/4	16 5/8	17		
SLEEVE	**15. Shoulder to elbow**	13 1/2	13 3/8	13 5/8	13 3/4 plus		
LENGTHS	**15a. Sleeve length (total)**	22 3/4	22 7/8	23 1/4	23 1/2		
	15b. Elbow to wrist	9 3/8	9 3/8	9 1/2	9 5/8		
SLEEVE	**16. Sleeve width at biceps**	11 5/8	11 7/8	12 1/4	12 7/8		
WIDTHS	**16a. Sleeve cap length to bic**	5 1/2	5 1/2	5 7/8	6		
	16b. Sleeve width at elbow	10	10 1/4 plus	10 5/8	11 plus		
	17. Waistline adjustments						
SKIRT	**18. Waist (skirt)**	**24**	**25**	**26**	**27 1/4 plus**		
WIDTH	1/2 waist measure	12	12 1/2	13	13 5/8		
	front waist	6 1/4	6 1/2	6 3/4	7 minus		
	back waist	5 3/4	6	6 1/4	6 5/8 plus		
	19. Hip 3" from waist	30 3/4	31 1/2	33	34 1/4		
	1/2 of 3" measure	15 3/8	15 3/4	16 1/2	17 5/8		
	front 3" from waist	7 3/4 plus	8	8 3/8	8 5/8 plus		
	back 3" from waist	7 1/2	7 3/4	8	8 3/8		
	20. Hip 7" from waist	34 1/4	35 1/8	36 1/4	38		
	1/2 of 7" measure	17 1/8	17 1/2	18 1/2	19		
	front 7" from waist	8 1/2 plus	8 3/4	9 plus	9 3/8		
	back 7" from waist	8 1/2	8 3/4 minus	9	9 1/2		
	21. Hip 9" from waist	**34 1/4**	**35 1/8**	**36 1/4**	**38**		
	1/2 of 9" measure	17 7/8 minus	18	18 1/8	19		
	front 9" from waist	8 1/2 plus	8 7/8	9 1/8	9 1/2		
	back 9" from waist	8 1/2	8 3/4	9	9 1/2		
If the measurement is 1/16 inch, it is shown as a plus or minus							

Courtesy of Vogue Patterns, Butterick Co., 161 Avenue of the Americas, NY, NY 10013

19

Industry Standard Dress Measurement Chart					
VOGUE 1004					
	Size	**14**	**16**	**18**	
BODICE	**1. High bust or chest**	**36**	**38**	**40**	
WIDTHS	**2. Bust (full)**	**38 7/8**	**41**	**43**	
	1/2 bust measure	19 3/8 plus	20 1/2	21 1/2	
	front tissue	10 1/4	10 5/8	11 1/4	
	back tissue	9 1/4 plus	9 3/4	10 1/4	
	3. Bust Tip Width	3 3/4	3 7/8	4	
	4. Front Width at notch	**7 1/2**	**7 3/4**	**8 1/2**	
	5. Shoulder width	**5 1/8**	**5 1/8 plus**	**5 3/8**	
	6. Back width at notch	8 3/8	8 5/8	9	
7. Total armhole	7 a & b. Total front & back armhole / underarm from dot at front & back width				
	7. Armhole	17 3/8	18 1/4	19	
	7a. Front armhole/underarm	8 3/4 / 2 3/4	9 1/8 / 2 7/8	9 1/2 / 3 1/8	
	7b. Back armhole/underarm	8 5/8 / 2 1/4	9 1/8 / 2 3/4	9 1/2 / 2 1/2	
	8.Neckline	15 3/8	15 3/4	16 1/8	
	8a. front neckline	4 1/2	4 5/8	4 3/4	
	8b. back neckline	3 1/8	3 1/4	3 1/4 plus	
BODICE	9. & 9a measurements are from center back neckline to bust symbol				
LENGTHS	**9.** Center back to bust line	14 1/4	14 5/8 plus	15 1/8	
	9a. Center back to waistline	21 1/8	21 1/2	22 plus	
	10. Center front bodice	14 7/8	15 1/8	15 3/8	
	11. Center back bodice	16 3/4	17	17 3/8	
	12. Side Seam	7 7/8	7 7/8	7 7/8	
SHOULDER	**13.** Front Slope	17 5/8 plus	18	18 1/2	
SLOPE	**14.** Back Slope	17 1/4 plus	17 3/8	17 7/8 plus	
SLEEVE	**15.** Shoulder to elbow	14 1/4	14 3/8	14 7/8	
LENGTHS	**15a.** Sleeve length (total)	23 3/8	24	24 3/4	
	15b. Elbow to wrist	9 1/8	9 5/8	9 3/4	
SLEEVE	**16.** Sleeve width at biceps	13 1/4	13 7/8	14 3/8	
WIDTHS	**16a.** Sleeve cap length to biceps	6 1/4	6 3/8	6 5/8	
	16b. Sleeve width at elbow	11 3/4	12 1/8	12 1/2	
	17. Waist adjustments				
SKIRT	**18.** Waist (skirt)	**29**	**31**	**32 3/4**	
WIDTH	1/2 waist measure	14 1/2	15 1/2	16 3/8	
	front waist	7 1/2 plus	8	8 3/8	
	back waist	7	7 1/2	8	
	19. Hip 3" from waist	35 3/4	37 3/4 plus	39 1/2	
	1/2 of 3" measure	17 7/8	18 7/8	19 3/4	
	front 3" from waist	9 1/8	9 5/8	10 plus	
	back 3" from waist	8 3/4	9 1/4	9 5/8 plus	
	20. Hip 7" from waist	39 3/4 minus	41 1/4	43 1/4	
	1/2 of 7" measure	19 7/8 minus	20 5/8	21 3/4	
	front 7" from waist	9 7/8	10 3/8	10 7/8	
	back 7" from waist	9 7/8 minus	10 1/4	10 3/4 plus	
	21. Hip 9" from waist	**39 3/4**	**41 3/4**	**43 1/2**	
	1/2 of 9" measure	19 7/8	20 7/8	21 3/4	
	front 9" from waist	9 7/8	10 3/8	10 7/8	
	back 9" from waist	9 7/8	10 3/8	10 7/8	
If the measurement is 1/16 inch, it is shown as a plus or minus					
Courtesy Of Vogue Patterns, Butterick Co., 161 Avenue Of the Americas, NY, NY 10013					

Industry Standard Dress Measurement Chart					
	VOGUE 1004				
	Size	**20**	**22**	**24**	
BODICE	**1. High bust or chest**	**42**	**44**	**46**	
WIDTHS	**2. Bust (full)**	**45**	**47 1/4**	**49 1/4**	
	1/2 bust measure	22 1/2	23 5/8	24 5/8	
	front tissue	11 3/4	12 1/4 plus	12 3/4 plus	
	back tissue	10 3/4	11 3/8	11 3/4	
	3. Bust Tip Width	4 1/8	4 1/4	4 3/8	
	4. Front Width at notch	**8 1/2**	**8 3/4**	**9 1/8**	
	5. Shoulder width	**5 1/2**	**5 5/8**	**5 3/4**	
	6. Back width at notch	9 1/4	9 5/8 plus	10	
7. Total armhole	7 a & b. Total front & back armhole / underarm from dot at front & back width				
	7. Armhole	19 3/4	20 1/2	21 1/4	
	7a. Front armhole/underarm	9 7/8 / 3 1/4	10 1/4 / 3 1/2	10 5/8 / 3 5/8	
	7b. Back armhole/underarm	9 7/8 / 2 3/4	10 1/4 / 2 7/8	10 5/8 / 3	
	8. Neckline	16 7/8	17 3/8	17 5/8 plus	
	8a. front neckline	4 7/8	5 1/8	5 1/4	
	8b. back neckline	3 3/8	3 1/2	3 1/2 plus	
BODICE	9. & 9a measurements are from center back neckline to bust symbol				
LENGTHS	**9.** Center back to bust line	15 1/2	16	16 1/4	
	9a. Center back to waistline	22 3/8	22 7/8 plus	23 1/8	
	10. Center front bodice	15 5/8	15 7/8	16 1/8	
	11. Center back bodice	17 5/8	18	18 1/4	
	12. Side Seam	7 7/8	7 7/8	7 7/8	
SHOULDER	**13.** Front Slope	18 3/4 plus	19 1/8	19 1/2	
SLOPE	**14.** Back Slope	18 1/8 plus	18 1/2	19 3/4	
SLEEVE	**15.** Shoulder to elbow	15 1/4	15 5/8	15 7/8 plus	
LENGTHS	**15a.** Sleeve length (total)	25 1/4	25 5/8	26 1/8	
	15b. Elbow to wrist	10	10 plus	10 1/8	
SLEEVE	**16.** Sleeve width at biceps	15	15 1/2	16 plus	
WIDTHS	**16a.** Sleeve cap length to biceps	6 7/8	7 1/8	7 1/4	
	16b. Sleeve width at elbow	13 1/8	13 1/2	13 7/8	
	17. Waistline adjustments				
SKIRT	**18.** Waist	**35 inch**	**36 3/4**	**39**	
WIDTH	1/2 waist measure	17 3/8 plus	18 3/8	19 1/2	
	front waist	8 1/2	9 3/8	10	
	back waist	8 7/8 plus	9	9 1/2	
	19. Hip 3" from waist	41 3/4	43 3/4	45 5/8	
	1/2 of 3" measure	20 7/8	21 3/4 plus	22 3/4	
	front 3" from waist	10 1/4	11 plu	11 1/2	
	back 3" from waist	10 5/8	10 3/4	11 1/4	
	20. Hip 7" from waist	45 1/2	47 1/4	49 3/8 plus	
	1/2 of 7" measure	22 3/4	23 1/2 plus	24 5/8 plus	
	front 7" from waist	1 3/8 minus	11 3/4 plus	12 3/8	
	back 7" from waist	10 5/8	11 3/4	12 1/4 plus	
	21. Hip 9" from waist	**45 3/4**	**47 5/8**	**49 7/8**	
	1/2 of 9" measure	22 7/8	23 3/4 plus	24 3/4 plus	
	front 9" from waist	11 3/8	11 7/8	12 3/8 plus	
	back 9" from waist	11 3/8 plus	11 7/8	12 3/8	
	If the measurement is 1/16 inch, it is shown as a plus or minus				
Courtesy Of Vogue Patterns, Butterick Co., 161 Avenue Of the Americas, NY, NY 10013					

Adjusting The Basic Dress Pattern To Your Measurements

The goal when adjusting the commercial basic pattern is to have as few changes as possible and still have a great fit.

One common adjustment women have when fitting is the bust line. Make sure you wear a well-fitted bra. If your bra does not fit close to your breastbone, it probably is not the correct size.

The average woman is a "C" cup or larger which requires an adjustment for a larger bust cup size. It is important to wear the correct size bra when your measurements are taken, during the tissue fitting and at the pin fitting.

Bra Size
The bra band size is determined by measuring under the bust line and adding four to five inches.

Numbers are from the dress measurement chart.
2a. Under-bust (your measurements)_____
Plus 4-5 inches equals band size _____.

The **bust cup** size is determined by the difference in the high bust measurement and the full bust measurement. 0" is an 'AA' cup, 1" is an 'A' cup, 2" is a 'B' cup, 3" is a 'C" cup, 4" is a 'D" cup, 5" is a "DD' cup.

Numbers are from the dress measurement chart.
2. Full Bust (your measurement) _____ **minus** the **1.** High Bust (your measurement)
_____**equals** your bra cup size _____
Since there are differences in how brands fit, visit a department store and have a bra fitting expert assist you in finding the perfect fitting bra before you begin your pattern fitting.

Front Bodice: The bust shaping adjustment is crucial for a good fit. **All commercial patterns are drafted for a B cup bra.** If your bust cup size is larger or smaller than a B cup, you must increase or decrease your patterns to fit your bust cup size.

The differences in the bust cup sizes are apparent when each bust cup size is layered as shown in sketch (sk1-1). It becomes apparent the change is in length as well as width and extends into the armhole.

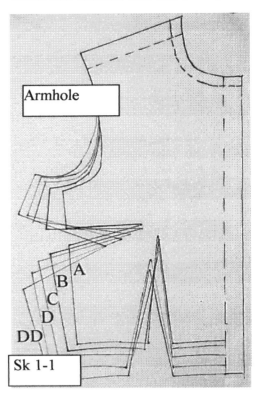

Some basic patterns, including Vogue, have front bodices with A, B, C, and D cup tissues. That can be confusing because all fashion patterns you will adjust using your basic pattern are drafted using a B cup. Use the B cup tissue and adjust it to fit your bust cup size making changes consistent when adjusting fashion patterns.

Option: Use the bust cup tissue that matches your bust cup. After it is adjusted for your figure differences, compare it with the B cup tissue. Note the changes to the B cup and make those changes to fashion patterns.

The changes for the bust cup size are illustrated for each bust cup size, sketches 3-1, 4-1, 5-1, and 6-1.

Pattern Adjustment Methods

The **seam method** of adjusting patterns is done by cutting the pattern along the seam line and lapping or spreading to adjust the seam.

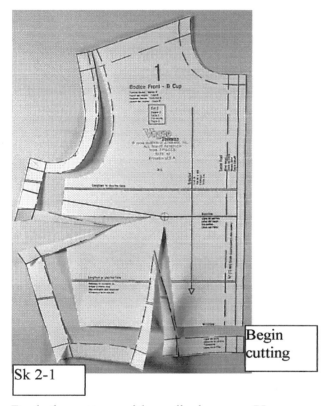

Sk 2-1

Begin cutting

Back the pattern with medical paper. Use removable glue stic (Refer to Fitting Tools) to hold the pattern in place until everything is adjusted. Pin the tissue to hold it firmly in place during the tissue fitting.

There are several ways to adjust patterns; slash and spread, pivoting the pattern and adding to the cutting edge are three methods that are commonly used. The **seam method** of adjusting patterns is the easiest and best way to adjust patterns. Anywhere an adjustment is needed the adjustment is done at the seam line. **All pattern adjustments in this workbook are shown using the seam method.** The length adjustments shown are done accurately at the seam line instead of at the lengthen/shorten lines on the pattern (sk 9-1 & 10-1).

B cup tissue adjusted for an A cup bra

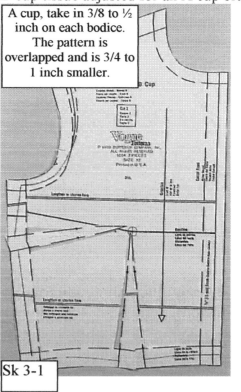

A cup, take in 3/8 to ½ inch on each bodice. The pattern is overlapped and is 3/4 to 1 inch smaller.

Sk 3-1

B cup tissue adjusted for a C cup bra

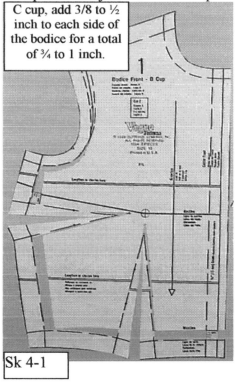

C cup, add 3/8 to ½ inch to each side of the bodice for a total of ¾ to 1 inch.

Sk 4-1

B cup tissue adjusted for a D cup bra

D cup, add ¾ to 1 inch to each side of the bodice for a total of 1/1/2 to 2 inches

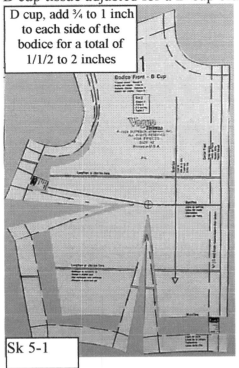

Sk 5-1

B cup tissue adjusted for a DD cup bra

DD cup, add 1 ¼- 1½ inches to each side of the bodice for a total of 21/2 to 3 inches.

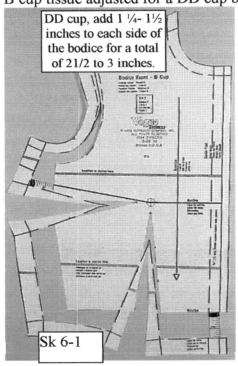

Sk 6-1

Wearing Ease
wearing ease is only enough ease to move and breathe and is added to your body measurements on the Measurement Chart.

Full Bust: 2 to 3 inches
Waist: 1 to 1 1/2 inches
Hip line: 2 inches
Reach room ease in bodice:
Front Width: 1/2 inch.
Back Width: 3/4 inch

Pattern Adjustment:
Keep in mind posture and body contours when adjusting patterns.
If the shoulders are sloped, square, broad, or tilt forward they affect the way the garment hangs and fits.
If the back is curved, flat, narrow or broad, it affects fit.
If the waist is tilted down in back or front or if one hip is high and large it affects the way a skirt or slack fits.
If a body is carrying extra weight the distribution of that weight affects areas where added fabric is needed.
Fabric will not travel, you must add or take away fabric so that it fits the body contours.

Example: When adjusting the side seams at the waistline, both decreasing the bodice waistline darts and adding to the side seams add width.

If you are full in the front waist, and don't need the bust shaping, decreasing the bodice waist dart and adding any extra width needed to the side seam is the solution.

If the back is flat, decreasing the back bodice dart will give extra room in the waist and decrease the shaping for a curved back.

Darts are used to shape, to add or decrease fullness and must end at the fullest part of the body. A dart that extends past the fullest part, removes fabric where it is needed, and adds fabric below the curve where it is not needed. Look closely at the curves of the body and shape darts to fit the curves.

The basic dress is fitted very closely to show your body differences from the industry standard. When adjusting commercial fashion patterns allow more ease to hide the body imperfections.

Pattern Size
Determine your pattern size by your measurements at your high bust, your shoulder and your front width.

Those measurements from the Dress Measurement Chart are:
1. High bust_____
4. Front width _____
5. Shoulder width _____

Compare your measurements with the dress sizes on the Dress Standard Flat Tissue Measurement Chart to choose your correct size pattern.

Your pattern size is _____.

Sequence of Pattern Adjustment
Bodice Length
Front Bodice
Back Bodice
Sleeve
Skirt

Always press the pattern before adjusting and again before you cut the fabric. Allow one-inch fitting seams at the shoulder, side seams, waistline and center front.

Bodice Length
Check the back bodice length (sk 7-1) and front bodice length (sk 8-1). The side seam length is only an extra guide in judging bodice length since there is no accurate body landmark for the underarm.

Raising or lowering the neckline also affects the center front and back lengths. Any neckline adjustments are done later in the sequence and checked at the tissue pin fitting with final adjustment at the muslin pin fitting.

Back bodice length

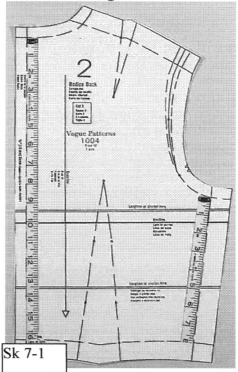

Sk 7-1

Front bodice length

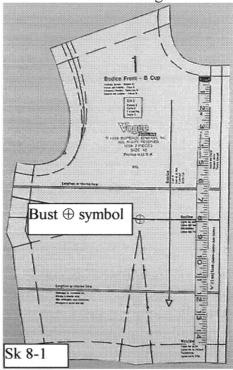

Bust ⊕ symbol

Sk 8-1

If both the front and back bodice needs to be adjusted in length (sk 9-1 and 10-1) make

the adjustments before adjusting the bust-line.
If only the front is short and your bust cup is larger than a 'B' cup, the bust cup adjustment will correct the front bodice.

To begin check your measurements with the measurements for **your size pattern** on the Dress Standard Flat Tissue Measurement Chart.

Numbers are from the dress measurement chart.
10. Center front bodice length (your measurements) _____ Tissue Center Front (from the flat measurement chart in your size) _____ lengthen or shorten_____

Cut the pattern at the seam-line and overlap to shorten the bodice back (sk 9-1).

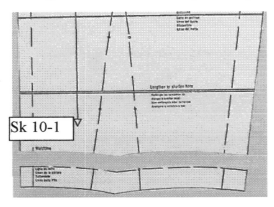

Numbers are from the dress measurement chart.
11. Center back bodice length (your measurements_____ Tissue Center Back (from the flat measurement chart) _____lengthen or shorten_____

Cut the pattern at the seam-line and spread to lengthen the bodice back (sk-10-1).

Sequence of pattern adjustment and your progress:
Bodice Length   **finished**
Front Bodice
Back Bodice
Sleeve
Skirt

Front Bodice
Compare your **width** measurements (sk 11-1) with the flat tissue measurements from the chart.

2. Full bust _____
2b. Bust cup size _____
3. Bust tip_____
4. Front width_____
5. Shoulder width_____
18. Waist (total)_____

Compare your **length** measurements (sk 12-1) with the flat tissue measurements from the chart.

9. Bust line ⊕ (center back to full bust) This is the bust line symbol from the tissue(⊕).
9a. Waistline (center back to front waistline)

Compare the measurements in your size from the flat tissue measurement chart before actually changing the pattern so you can see how your body differs from the basic pattern. Most changes can be accomplished at the same time (sk 13-1).

The bodice front is adjusted for the Bra bust cup size Error! Bookmark not defined. **before it is adjusted for the full bust width.**

Numbers are from the dress measurement chart.
Full Bust Width (2) (back & front) of the adjusted pattern must equal your measurement plus wearing ease (sk 11-1 & 15-1).
Use 2 inches of ease for a close fit or 3 inches of ease for a looser fit.

2. Full Bust (your measurements) _____ + 2-3 inches of ease =_____. One half the measurement of full bust with ease is _____
2b. Bust cup size_____

A cup adjustment minus 3/8 to ½ inch (sk 3-1)
B cup-no adjustment
C cup adjustment plus 3/8 to ½ inch (sk 4-1)
D cup adjustment plus ¾ to 1 inch (sk 5-1)
DD cup adjustment plus 1 ¼ to 1 1/2 inches (sk 6-1)

Check front widths

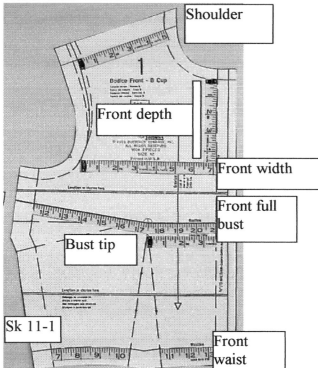

Numbers are from the dress measurement chart.
Bust tip Width (3) Divide the distance from bust tip to bust tip in half and measure from the center front of the pattern to the bust line symbol ⊕. The waistline dart must be in line with your bust tip and both the waistline dart and the side seam dart must end from ½ to 1 inch (small sizes less, large sizes more) from the bust ⊕. (sk 11-1)

3. Bust Tip Width ____1/2____ the dart is correct or needs to be moved this amount____

Numbers are from the dress measurement chart.
Front width (4) measured armhole to armhole where the arm attaches to the body (sk 11-1). (The bust cup size affects this measurement).

4. Front Width_____ (your measurement)
1/2_____ plus ¼ inch ease _____.
Tissue Front Width _____plus or minus_____

Numbers are from the dress measurement chart.
Shoulder width (5) is from the neckline to the armhole at the shoulder (sk11-1). Measure the tissue on the front bodice. The Vogue tissue has three shoulder seam lines; narrow, standard & broad marked on the pattern. Use the standard (middle) line.

5. Shoulder width _____(your measurement)
Tissue shoulder width ____ plus or minus
_____

Numbers are from the dress measurement chart.
Total waistline (18) (back & front) (sk11-1 & 15-1)

18. Waist _____(your measurement) plus 1 to 1 ½ inches ease. 1/2 of the waist _____
Tissue waist _____Plus or minus
_____

Numbers are from the dress measurement chart.

Bodice lengths (9 and 9a) correctly adjust the side bust dart placement, the bust shaping and the bodice length (sk12-1).

Front bodice length (9) is measured from the center back neckline (prominent bone at neckline) to the bust line.

Numbers are from the dress measurement chart.

9. Bust Line (CB to full bust⊕) _____ (your measurements Tissue length _____ raise or lower _____ .

Numbers are from the dress measurement chart.

Front waistline length (9a) is measured from the center back neckline (prominent bone at neckline) over the bust-line to the waist at the waist bust dart.

9a. To waistline _____ (your measurements) Tissue length _____ raise or lower _____

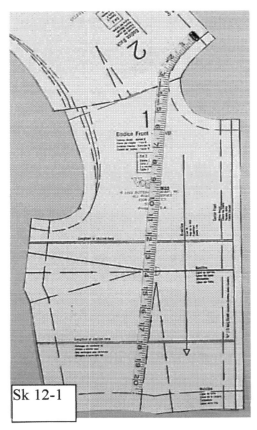

Sk 12-1

After all the measurements are compared with the pattern, you can see what

changes must be made in width and length for the pattern to fit your bust.

Prepare the pattern by cutting along the seam lines. Begin at the waistline at center front (sk 2-1), cut around the darts, to the armhole notch. Then cut through the center of the dart from the cutting line to the point. Don't cut through the point!

Tip! *Reinforce darts with tape on under side before cutting.*

Clipping the seam allowance from cutting edge up-to-but-not-through the stitching line allows the seam to lie flat. The pattern must be backed.

Tip! *Twenty-inch wide paper purchased from a medical supply store works well.*

Read the example used to illustrate the changes and then adjust your front bodice in width and length.

Example 1: Sue is a client from several years ago. I am using her bust cup changes to illustrate how to change your pattern to fit your bust cup size and your full bust measurement. Sue's example is printed in blue to differentiate it from the directions for your pattern adjustment.

Sue fits best in a size 12 pattern at the shoulders and neckline. She wears a DD cup bra, and is full in the waist. Her full bust measurement is 41 inches and her waistline is 30 ¼ inches. Her bust tip, and front width fit the size 12 flat tissue measurements when adjusted for a DD cup.

The bodice front and back patterns were cut along the seam lines and bust darts to make adjustments for the bust cup size, the dart placement and the bodice front length and width (Sue's example sk 13-1 & 14-1).

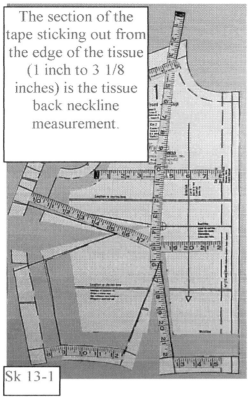

The section of the tape sticking out from the edge of the tissue (1 inch to 3 1/8 inches) is the tissue back neckline measurement.

Sk 13-1

The front pattern is lengthened to reflect the DD cup bra. The bust and waistline are increased to reflect her bust and waist. The skirt and sleeve will also be changed to correspond with the changes to the bodice.

Sue's **Width** (2.) Full Bust width⊕
Full Bust (Sue's measurement) is 41 plus 3 inches of ease equals 44. One-half the measurement of full bust with ease is 22.

A size 12 B cup tissue pattern is 18 ½ (from the flat tissue measurement chart) plus the 1 ½ adjustment for the DD bust cup (her bust cup size) equals 20 on half the tissue or 40 for the full tissue.

The pattern is now adjusted for the Sue's DD bust cup (40 inches) but it is still short of the needed amount for her full bust width (44 inches). Subtracting the 40 from the 44 equals 4 inches. Divide the 4 inches by 4 and add 1 inch to the front tissue (sk12-1) and 1 inch to the back tissue (sk13-1) at the bust line. The pattern now equals a total of 44 inches for Sue's total full bust measurement.

Tip! *If you are working with the full pattern measurement, divide the amount to adjust by four and add or subtract at the side seam. If you are working with half the pattern divide the amount to adjust by two and add or subtract at the side seam.*

Numbers are from the dress measurement chart.
18. Waist 30 ¼ (Sue's measurement) plus 1 to 1 ½ inches ease equals 31 1/4
Tissue waist 27 ¼ (from the flat tissue measurement chart) Sue's waist is 31 ¼ minus 27 ¼ equals a 4 inch increase.

Convert from the full waist to half waist to adjust the tissue.
One half of the waist is 15 5/8 increase the waist 2 inches. Add one inch to the front waist and 1 inch to the back waist.

Length
Numbers are from the dress measurement chart.
9. Bust Line (CB to full bust⊕) 14 7/8 inches (Sue's front length measurements) Tissue measurement is 14 inches. Lower the bust line 7/8 inch (sk 13-1).

9a. Waistline Line (CB to waist) 22 1/2 (Sue's back length measurements) tissue measurement is 20 3/4 inches. Lower the waistline 1 ¼ inches (sk 13-1).
Both the change in width for the DD cup, the full bust line, and total waistline are reflected on the pattern (sk 12-1 & 13-1). The adjustment for a DD cup bra is shown by the line inside the seam allowance (sk 12-1). The additional width was needed for the full bust measurement after the bust cup adjustment and was added evenly on the front and back side seams (sk 13-1 & 14-1). Since 1 inch was added at the side seam the same amount will be added to the skirt waistline and to the armhole of the sleeve (sk 37-1).
The length measurement reflects the lower bust line and the longer front length (sk 13-1) needed by Sue.
After adjusting, check all the widths of the bodice front including the shoulder to be sure they correspond with the body

measurements plus wearing ease. If the front bodice side seam length does not exactly match the back side-seam length, adjust the front side length by increasing or decreasing the side seam dart.

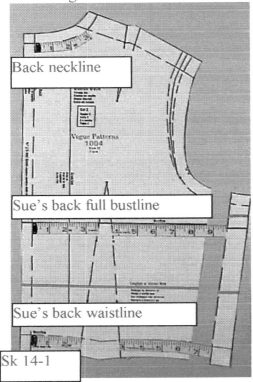

Back neckline

Sue's back full bustline

Sue's back waistline

Sk 14-1

Sue's bodice is adjusted for her bust cup size and her full bust measurement.

Follow the example and adjust your pattern as needed in the following areas:
2. Full bust
2a. Bust cup size
3. Bust tip
4. Front width
5. Shoulder _____
18. Total waist _____

Sequence of pattern adjustment and your progress:
Bodice Length	**finished**
Front Bodice	**finished**
Back Bodice	
Sleeve	
Skirt	

Now adjust the remainder of the pattern in numerical order beginning with the back shoulder (5).

Bodice Back
The center back length has been checked. If needed it was adjusted. Check it again at the tissue pin fitting and check for shrug room at the muslin pin fitting. Compare your shoulder and back width measurements with the pattern (sk 15-1).

Back Widths

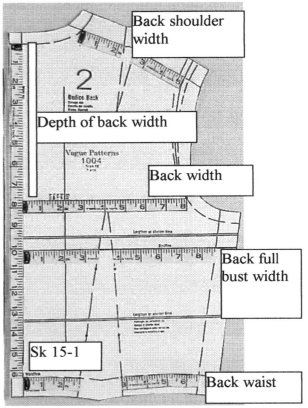

Back shoulder width

Depth of back width

Back width

Back full bust width

Sk 15-1

Back waist

Numbers are from the dress measurement chart.

Shoulder (5)
Garments hang from the shoulders so the fit of garments in the shoulder and armhole is crucial for good fit and comfort. There must be room to move the arms forward and backward and to shrug the shoulders. **The shoulder seam must lie exactly on the top of the shoulder at the shoulder joint.** To establish the shoulder joint move the arm up and down to feel and mark the shoulder pivot point. A weighted string lying from the

neckline along the shoulder and hanging plumb over the shoulder will help pinpoint this body landmark. (Refer to Taking Measurements Picture 7-1).

Your front just below the shoulder is hollow. Your back just below the shoulder is rounded.

The back shoulder is adjusted slightly wider (1/8 to1/4 inch) and is eased onto the front shoulder to reflect the body shape.

5. Shoulder width (your measurement)_____
pattern _____plus or minus _____
Add 1/8 to ¼ to the back shoulder.

Shoulder Differences

Common shoulder changes are broad shoulder (sk 16-1), narrow shoulders (sk 17-1), square shoulders (sk 18-1), and sloped shoulders (sk 19-1). The most common alteration is for the forward shoulder (sk 20-1).

Most shoulder changes require changes to the sleeve cap. The sleeve changes are illustrated in the sleeve adjustments (sk 34-1 through sk 43-1).

Broad shoulders

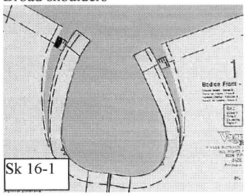

Sk 16-1

Broad shoulders need extra width added to both the front and the back. Usually the broad shoulder adjustment does not require changes to the sleeve.

Narrow shoulders

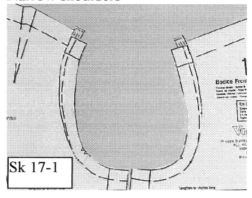

Sk 17-1

Remove width on both the front and back shoulder which makes the armhole longer (sk 17-1).
Change the sleeve (sk 39-1) to reflect the longer armhole.

The armhole of both garment (sk 26-1) and the sleeve (sk 43-1) may need to be raised.

Square shoulders

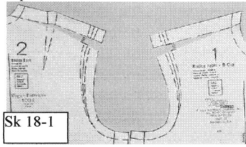

Sk 18-1

Square shoulders are indicated when a garment neckline does not lie flat and the shoulders appear snug. During the tissue fitting open the shoulder seam and pin fit the shoulder seam allowing enough room for the shoulders. The neckline will then fit the body.

Cut the tissue along the shoulder seam and spread the tissue (sk 18-1) to match the addition to the shoulder that was added at the pin fitting. Change the sleeve to correspond (sk 39-1).

Sloped shoulders

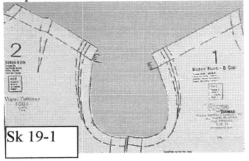

Sk 19-1

The garment neckline fits. There is excess length in the shoulder and upper sleeve. Open the shoulder and pin fit the shoulder seam until it fits the shoulder. Mark the new seam and adjust the tissue by cutting along the seam-line and overlapping the seam at the shoulder armhole junction (sk 19-1). The corresponding sleeve change is (sk 36-1) shortening the cap. Be sure you have adequate ease in the cap when it is lowered. The cap must have from ½ to ¾ inch ease on both the back and front cap. Pin fit the cap at the muslin pin fitting.

Forward shoulder

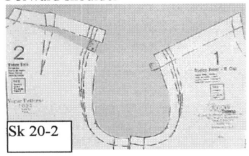

Sk 20-2

Garments that ride to the back are uncomfortable to wear. You constantly feel as if you need to pull the front of the garment back into place. Release the sleeve, open the shoulder seam, establish the shoulder pivot point, pin fit the shoulder seam.

The sleeve adjustment is seen on sk 36-1. Reset the sleeve so the cross-grain line is hanging parallel to the floor.

Cut the tissue along the shoulder seam and spread the tissue to match the addition to the muslin. The front bodice may or may not need adjustment (sk 20-1).

Back Width (6)

Back width is measured from armhole to armhole where the arm attaches to the body. On the tissue, the back width is shown on (sk 15-1). Measure the depth of the back width **(6a)** as shown by the bar on sketch 21-1. If you need more room at the back width, add just to the back armhole or also add to the side seam (sk 21-1) and to the back sleeve (sk 37-1).

Numbers are from the dress measurement chart.
6. Back width (your measurement)_____ **6a**
distance from CB neckline _____ divide the
back width by half_____ add 3/8 –1/2 inch
ease equals _____
Tissue measurement _____ plus or minus ___

Look at the shape of the back. Is it curved or very straight? The pattern has darts which give room for a somewhat curved back (sk 15-2 & 21-2).
When a back is straight or flat decrease the darts.

Increase the darts, especially the shoulder dart if the shoulders are rounded.

If the shoulder is curved and the back is very erect decrease the back bodice dart and leave the shoulder dart as it is on the tissue.

If one shoulder is higher and protrudes more than the other shoulder, the dart for the higher larger shoulder will be larger and may be longer. The appearance of the darts should be as similar as possible. Some adjustment for the larger shoulder can be made in the center back seam.

Broad back

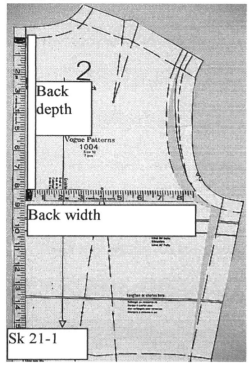

Sk 21-1

Numbers are from the dress measurement chart.

Armhole Depth (7)

Measurement of front and back armhole (7a and 7b) is helpful in judging the shoulder, the placement of the shoulder seam and the depth of the armhole (sk 22-1 & 23-1) is especially important for tall or petite figures that may need adjustments in the armhole as well as the regular lengthen/shorten areas.

On the basic fitting garment, the underarm should be as high as it can be and still be comfortable. On fashion garments, the underarm position varies. It is very helpful to know the armhole depth of a closely fitted garment so that you can judge fashion garments.

Check the armhole depth from shoulder to the notch or dot as shown by the bars (sk 22-1) and then measure the remaining area that is the underarm (sk 23 1).

Front and back armhole length

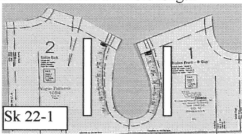

Sk 22-1

Numbers are from the dress measurement chart.

7a. Front armhole to crease_____ (your measurement) underarm_____
Tissue front armhole to dot or notch _____
underarm_____ lengthen or shorten_____

7b. Back armhole to crease____ (your measurement)
Tissue back armhole to dot or notch _____
underarm_____ Lengthen or shorten_____

Underarm

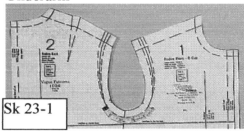

Sk 23-1

Armhole lengthened

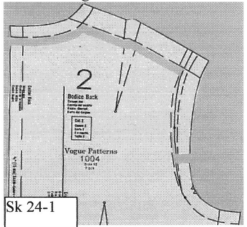

Sk 24-1

Armhole shortened, pattern overlapped

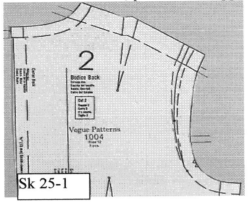

Sk 25-1

Under Arm Adjustment (sk 26-1)
The closer a garment fits the higher the armhole must be to insure movement. If it is cut too high, it can always be lowered. If it is not high enough you have only a 5/8 seam to use to raise the armhole.

Tip: *Cut it higher and check at the pin fitting. If too high simply stitch it lower and trim the seam line (sk 26-1 bodice and sk 38-1 sleeve).*

Raise the armhole ½ inch on bodice and on the sleeve.

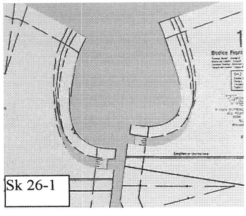

Sk 26-1

Neckline (8)
The jewel neckline should fit comfortably and lie at the hollow of the front neckline and at the prominent bone at the back neckline. If the neckline is too high or too low, alter by lowering (sk 27-1 & 30-1) or raising (sk 28-1& 29-1). A senior figure may need the front lowered and the back raised (sk 30-1 & 31-1).

Numbers are from the dress measurement chart.
8. Neckline (your measurement) _____ tissue measurement _____ Plus or minus_____

8a. Front neckline (your measurement) _____ tissue measurement _____ Plus or minus

_____

Stand the tape on edge to measure the curved neckline seam.

8b. Back neckline (your measurement) _____ tissue measurement _____ Plus or minus

_____

Changes to the neckline will affect the collar and neckline facings when adjusting fashion patterns. If the collar is shaped, the changes must be done to the same area of the collar as was done to the neckline.

Lower back neckline, pattern is overlapped.

Sk 27-1

Raised Back neckline

Sk 28-1

Raised front neckline

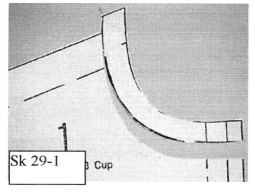

Sk 29-1   B Cup

Lowered front neckline-pattern is overlapped

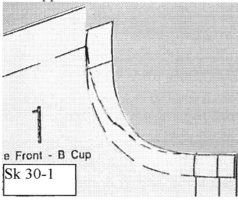

e Front - B Cup

Sk 30-1

Back neckline & shoulder raised

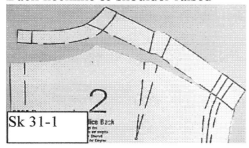

Sk 31-1   lice Back

Bodice Lengths

Check again if the neckline was adjusted.

Numbers are from the dress measurement chart.

9. Bust line of front tissue measured from center back has been adjusted and is not affected by the neckline adjustment.

10. Center front length _____

Center front length is used as guideline for adjusting the bodice length. Number 9 is the primary length adjustment for the bodice front.

11. Center back length _____

Center back length is used as a guideline along with the shoulder slope measurements to determine the back length. The bodice lengths are checked at the tissue fitting and the muslin pin fittings.

Shoulder Slopes (13 & 14)

The shoulder slope measurements (sk 32-1 & 33-1) help judge the length of the bodice and the fit through the shoulders. If the bodice tissues measure shorter than the slope measurement after the width, length, and shoulder adjustments are completed recheck your adjustments.

When the problem is not apparent, add extra seam allowance at the shoulder and waistline, check at the tissue pin fitting and do the final adjustment at the muslin pin fitting.

Measure the front shoulder slope

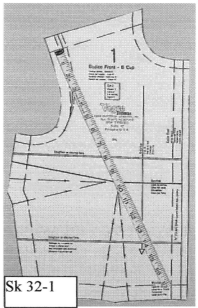

Sk 32-1

Numbers are from the dress measurement chart.

13. Front slope R_____ L_____ (your measurement)

Tissue pattern_____ Plus or minus _____

Measure the back shoulder slope

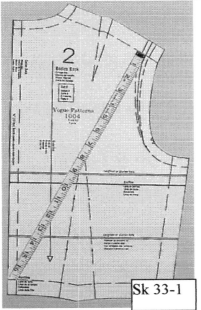

Sk 33-1

14. Back slope R_____ L_____ (your measurement)
Tissue pattern_____ Plus or minus _____

Sequence of pattern adjustment and your progress:

Bodice Length	**finished**
Front Bodice	**finished**
Back Bodice	**finished**
Sleeve	
Skirt	

Sleeve (15)

The sleeve must hang from the shoulder with the straight of grain perpendicular and the crosswise grain parallel to the floor.

Always add a crosswise grain line in the cap of the sleeve midway between the cap and the biceps line (sk 34-1). The shoulder determines how the sleeve will be set into the armhole. The crosswise grain line is invaluable in setting in the sleeve. **Ignore the notches and dots and set the sleeve into the armhole with the cross grain line parallel to the floor.**

Numbers are from the dress measurement chart.
Sleeve Lengths (15)

Check the length of the sleeve pattern from the shoulder to the wrist on the back of the pattern (sk 34-1). The elbow dart should be at the elbow and the bottom of the sleeve should be at the wrist bone with the arm bent. Lengthen or shorten the sleeve in the area needed (sk 35-1 & 36-1).

Numbers are from the dress measurement chart.
15. Outside arm length (your measurement)_____ Tissue outside arm length_____ shorten or lengthen ___ (sk 34-1)

15a. Shoulder to elbow (your measurement)_____ Tissue from shoulder to elbow _____ shorten or lengthen ___(sk 34-1)

15b. Elbow to wrist _____ Tissue from elbow to wrist_____ shorten or lengthen
(sk 34-1)

Sleeve lengths and widths

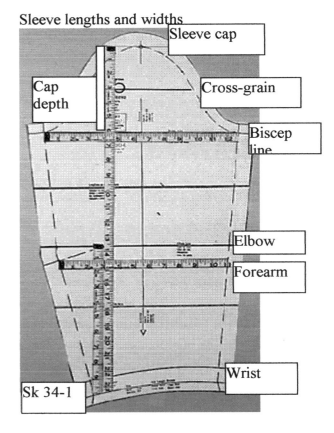

Sleeve cap

Cap depth

Cross-grain

Biscep line

Elbow

Forearm

Wrist

Sk 34-1

Lengthen sleeve above or below elbow

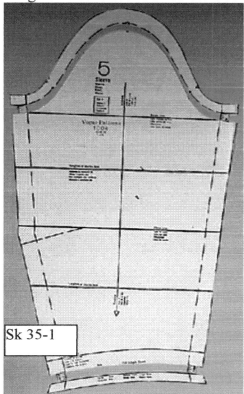

Sk 35-1

Shorten sleeve above or below elbow

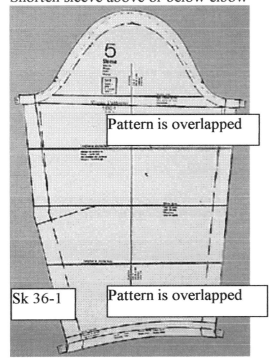

Pattern is overlapped

Sk 36-1

Pattern is overlapped

Numbers are from the dress measurement chart.

Sleeve Widths (16)

Check the sleeve width at the underarm (biceps line) on the tissue (sk 34-1). If the sleeve is not wide enough add to the sleeve width.

First, add the amount that was added to the bodice side seams (sk 13-1 & 14-1). The sleeve addition (sk 37-1) must match the bodice.

Second, when more width is needed, add it as in sketch 38-1. This prevents the sleeve cap from becoming too long to fit the armhole. It also lowers the sleeve cap.

It is much safer to mark the lower stitching line, cut the cap to the original height, and pin fit the sleeve. Cut off any extra fabric on the cap after the pin fitting.

16. Sleeve width at bicep (your measurement)_____ pattern _____plus or minus _____

16a Depth of cap, full arm to the shoulder line (your measurement)_____ on pattern measure from the sleeve cap to the bicep line _____ plus or minus _____

If the cap is lowered (sk 38-1 & 40-1)mark the lowered seam line and pin fit before cutting off the excess; this ensures adequate fabric on the cap to pin fit the sleeve.

16b. Forearm (your measurement) _____ pattern _____ plus or minus _____

If the forearm is heavily muscled, you may need extra width at the elbow and just below the elbow. Add to the back of the sleeve (sk 38-1) or only the elbow area can be increased.

Number **16c** the wrist measurement and **16d** the hand measurements from the dress measurement chart are used to adjust fashion patterns.

Adding to the full arm or bicep as shown in sketch 37-1 lengthens the total sleeve cap. Adding to the full arm or bicep as shown in sketch 38-1 does not lengthen the total sleeve cap.

Sleeve width added only to body of sleeve.

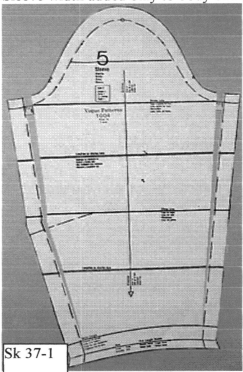

Sk 37-1

Sleeve width added to cap & the body of the sleeve.

Pattern is overlapped

Sk 38-1

Pattern is overlapped

Sleeve Cap Differences

The cap of the sleeve must be adjusted to correspond with any shoulder adjustment. **The sleeve cap must be ½ to ¾ inch larger than the front armhole and be ½ to ¾ inch larger than the back armhole. This allows 1 -1½ inch of minimum ease in the sleeve cap.**

Tip! *Stand your tape on edge to measure the curved armhole and sleeve cap.*

Sleeve cap raised

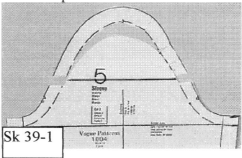

Sk 39-1

The sleeve cap must be raised (sk 39-1) when the shoulder is narrowed (sk 17-1) and when the shoulders are adjusted for square shoulder (sk 18-1).

The sleeve cap is lowered (sk 40-1) when the shoulders are sloped (sk 19-1).

Sleeve cap shortened

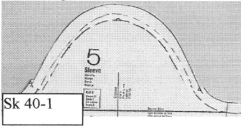

Sk 40-1

Forward shoulder adjustment to the sleeve

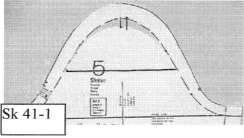

Sk 41-1

The forward shoulder (sk 20-1) is a very common adjustment. It lengthens only the back armhole so only the back sleeve is lengthened (sk 41-1). The sleeve is pin fit into the armhole making sure the cross-grain line is parallel to the floor.

Broad back adjustment for a sleeve

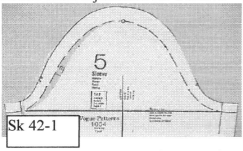

Sk 42-1

The back sleeve cap is widened (sk 42-1) to correspond with the width added to the back armhole (sk 21-1). These two small adjustments usually give adequate room to reach forward and cross your arms.

Armhole raised

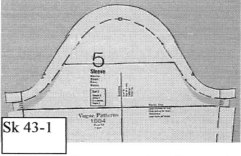

Sk 43-1

This is a safety precaution that can be used instead of testing the fashion pattern with a muslin test garment.
Raise the garment armhole (sk 26-1), the sleeve (sk 43-1), and raise the cap (sk 39-1). If the armhole or the cap is too high they can be lowered and the excess fabric can be trimmed after the pin fitting.

Sequence of pattern adjustment and your progress:

Bodice Length	**finished**
Front Bodice	**finished**
Back Bodice	**finished**
Sleeve	**finished**
Skirt	

Skirt
Waistline Adjustments (17)
Numbers are from the dress measurement chart.
A skirt hangs from the waistline. Waistline adjustments must be made for posture, pelvic tilt and extra weight. The adjustments include a prominent tummy, a low front waist, a low (sway) back, a prominent derriere, and uneven hips. The adjustments are made at the waistline seam, checked at the tissue fitting with a final check at the muslin pin fitting

Numbers are from the dress measurement chart.
17. Center back _____ Center front _____
             Difference _____
     Left side _____ Right side _____
             Difference _____

Figure Differences

Prominent Tummy

The center front to the floor measures longer than the center back to the floor and the tummy when seen on the profile is significant.

Raise the center front waistline seam (sk 44-1) the amount of the difference between center front and center back.

Raise the center front waistline

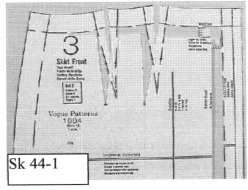

Sk 44-1

The raised seam will increase the center front and give more room for the tummy. If needed, an extra dart can be added to the waistline of the skirt.

Low Front Waist

Pelvic tilt or weight gain has resulted in a low front waistline. The front of all garments are too long.

Lower the center front (sk 45-1). Use caution when you lower a seam. It cannot be raised without adequate seam allowance. Mark the lower seam and allow extra seam allowance for further adjustment at the pin fitting. It can easily be removed if necessary.

Lower the waistline seam at center front

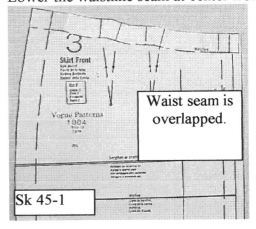

Waist seam is overlapped.

Sk 45-1

Extend the original center front seam to the cutting line (45-1).

Low (sway) Back

The pelvic tilt or posture makes the back shorter than the front. There is excess fabric below the waistband or waistline seam.

Lower the waistline seam at center back

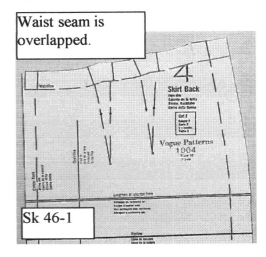

Waist seam is overlapped.

Sk 46-1

Lower the center back seam from center back to the original side seam (sk 46-1). Extend the original center back seam to the cutting line. Use caution when you lower a seam. It cannot be raised without adequate seam allowance. Mark the lower seam and allow extra seam allowance for further adjustment at the pin fitting.

Prominent Derriere

If the back length from the waist to the floor measures longer than the front length from the waist to the floor, and on the profile you can see a significant derriere, raise the waistline seam at the center back (sk 47-1).

Raise the waistline seam at center back

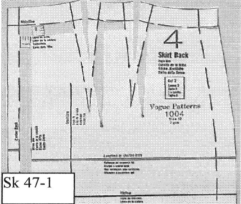

Sk 47-1

The raised seam will increase the center back and give more room for the derriere. If needed, the darts can be deepened and lengthened or an extra dart can be added to the waistline of the skirt. If there is excess fabric in the dart area, the dart legs can curve outward (convex) to remove excess fabric below the waist and still give room for the derriere (refer to chapter 3 Adjusting Darts).

Uneven Hip

One hip measures longer from the waist to the floor than the other hip. This is a very common figure difference.

Raise the waistline at the side seam (sk 48-1) the difference measured between the right side and the left side. The hip that is high is usually larger and will need more width at the hipline.

The pattern waist seam line is the low side; the raised seam allowance is the high side (sk 48-1 and close-up sk 49-1). The waist and side seam are evaluated at the tissue fitting and perfected at the pin fitting. The goal is to have enough seam allowance at waist and hip for the high large hip. The

center front and back seam must be at the body's center points. After the pin fitting, permanently mark the tissue.

Uneven hip adjustment

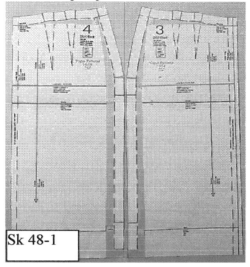

Sk 48-1

Tip! *Put Removable tape on the seam lines and mark the right side with a red pencil and the left side with a green pencil.*

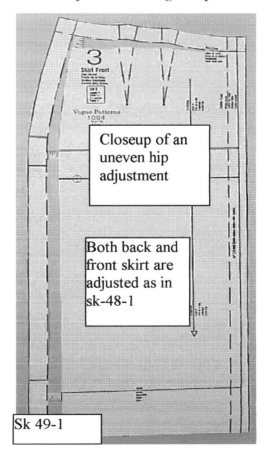

Closeup of an uneven hip adjustment

Both back and front skirt are adjusted as in sk-48-1

Sk 49-1

Skirt Widths (18-21)

Before adjusting the waistline measurement, evaluate the amount needed. Some adjustment can be made in the darts and the remainder at the side seams depending on your curves. The skirt waistline should be ½ -1 inch larger than the bodice waistline and should be eased on the bodice. An accentuated hip curve requires more ease.

Skirt widths

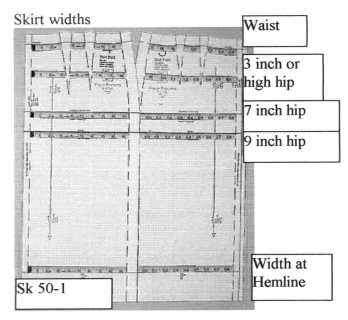

Waist

3 inch or high hip

7 inch hip

9 inch hip

Width at Hemline

Sk 50-1

Mark the distance from the waistline on the side seams at 3-7-9 inches (sk-50-1). The pattern must be adjusted to your measurements plus the wearing ease allowed.

18. Waist (your measurement plus ease from your measurement chart) _____ ½ of waist_____
Flat tissue measurement from chart_____
difference_____ divides by 2.

Add needed increase at the side seams (sk 51-2). The same amount that was added to the bodice (sk 13-1 & 14-1) can easily be added to the skirt. If more adjustment is needed, make the darts smaller or larger (sk 51-1).

19. 3" From waist + ease _____ ½
_____ flat tissue measurement from chart _____ plus or minus
_____Divide by two _____Adjust the side seams.

The front darts and the back side-dart should end at the high hip (sk 50-1). The high hip is the fullest part of the hip and stomach curve. Darts give fullness, if you aren't very rounded decrease the depth of the dart especially if you need a larger waistline than the pattern has allowed (sk 52-1 & 53-1). If you are very rounded and need more shape make the darts deeper or add another dart.

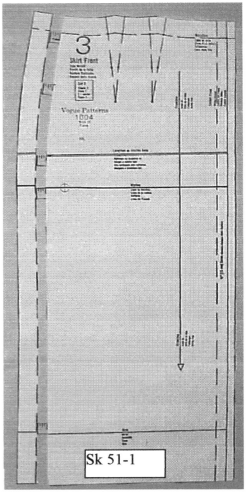

Sk 51-1

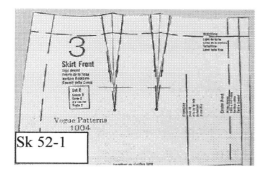

Sk 52-1

The front darts can be shortened to end at the fullest curve of the tummy and the dart legs can be curved inward (convex) to give more room over the rounded stomach (sk-52-1).

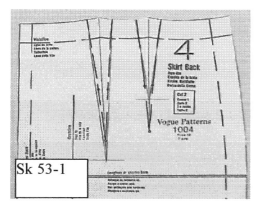

Sk 53-1

The back dart closest to the center back seam gives shape for the derriere. It must end at the fullest curve (sk 53-1). The back hip dart can be shortened to end at the hip curve. The dart legs can be curved inward to give more hip room (Sk 53-1). If the derriere is significant, the legs can curve outward (convex) to remove excess fabric below the waist.

The shape and length of the darts must fit your curves. Review Adjusting Darts.

Numbers are from the dress measurement chart.
20. 7" From waist + ease _____ ½ _____ flat tissue measurement from chart _____ plus or minus _____Divide by 2 _____Adjust the side seams.

Numbers are from the dress measurement chart.
21. 9" From waist + ease _____ ½ _____ flat tissue measurement from chart _____ plus or minus _____Divide by two _____Adjust the side seams.

The hip may be larger below or above the nine-inch mark on the skirt.
Numbers are from the dress measurement chart.
21a. Hip at the largest _____
21b. Distance from waistline_____

Measurement from the dress measurement chart
21c. Tape slips off hip line _____

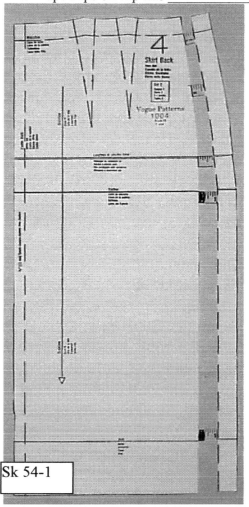

Sk 54-1

Additions to the hipline can vary from waist to hip but must stay the same from the largest part of the hip to the hemline (sk 54-1). Additions are done evenly to the back and front skirt on the side seams.

Numbers are from the dress measurement chart.

Skirt Length (9d)
The muslin is usually made knee length.
(9d). Numbers 9b, 9c, 9e and 9f from the dress measurement chart are used to adjust the length of fashion patterns.

This completes adjusting your basic pattern.

Pin the tissue together (Pic 25-1 & 26-1) and do the tissue fitting with your friend to assist you.

Tissue Fitting the Dress Basic Pattern

Tissue fitting is a valuable way to check the pattern adjustments you have made without actually making up the dress in fabric. It involves pinning or taping the backed pattern pieces together, usually half a garment (Pic 25-1 & 26-1), trying it on, evaluating the fit and making any necessary changes until you are happy with the pattern. If your right and left sides are noticeably different make a full tissue and tissue fit the sides individually. Any needed changes are made on the tissue before cutting and sewing the fitting muslin saving time and expense.

Prepare the Pattern

Use a combination of pins and "Scotch Brand Removable Magic Tape" to fasten the tissue together with seam line on seam line leaving the seam allowance at the seam junctions free. Also, pin and/or tape the darts. It is easiest to fold one seam allowance to the inside (Pic 25-1); clipping if needed, and lap it over the seam allowance on the matching pattern piece. Pinning at the beginning and the end of a seam holds it more securely than tape. Pinning with the head of the pin at the beginning of a seam will prevent the pin from jabbing you during the tissue fitting.

- Pin all the darts.
- Pin the bodice front and back together at the sides and shoulders.
- Pin the front and back skirt together at the side seams, pin up the hem.
- Pin the bodice to the skirt at the waistline.
- Pin a seam tape or narrow ribbon long enough to go around your waist and tie together at the waistline to the pattern. Pin the center of the ribbon to the side seam to distribute the ribbon equally around the waistline.
- Pin the sleeve together leaving it open enough for the hand to slip through the

sleeve opening. Pin the 5/8" seam allowance on the bottom of the sleeve flat.

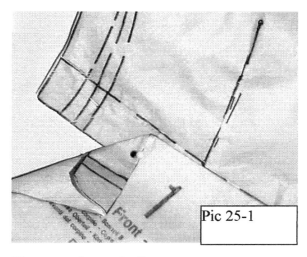

Pic 25-1

Tissue ready to pin fit

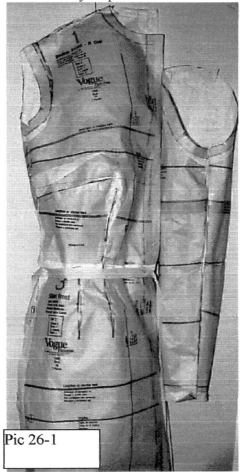

Pic 26-1

Courtesy of Vogue Patterns, Butterick Co., 161 Avenue of the Americas, NY, NY 10013

Prepare for Tissue fitting the Basic
Try the tissue on over the undergarments (bra, support garment, panty hose, or panties, and if desired a slip) that you wore when your measurements were taken. Put the drapery cord around your neck at your desired jewel neckline (Pic 35-1).

Tissue fitting
Slip the tissue on your body. Tie the ribbon around your waist. Pin the pattern to your bra at the bust line and to your undergarments at the hip line, front and back. Put the plumb line belt on the waist (Pic 35-1).

Evaluate Your Pattern
The basic fitting dress is closely fitted. Vertical seams should hang perpendicular to the floor. The cross grain lines should be parallel to the floor. Check them with the plumb line belt (Pic 35-1). If they don't hang straight, adjust the tissue at the shoulder on the bodice and at the waistline on the skirt until they hang correctly
Follow the sequence that was used on your basic as listed below:

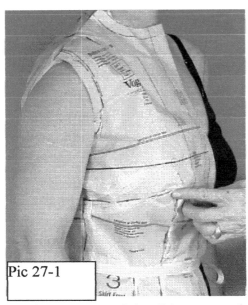
Pic 27-1

Bodice Length: If the ribbon around the tissue is at your waistline, and you can shrug your shoulders without unduly straining the pattern, the bodice length is correct.

Bust line: Both bust darts should point to the bust, end before the fullest part of the bust and provide adequate bust shaping (Pic 27-1). The pattern should reach to center front and center back in the bust area. If it doesn't, let out the side seams or increase the bust cup adjustment.

Shoulders: The shoulder seam should lie at the top of the shoulder and end at the shoulder joint (Pic 29-1). If needed, redraw the shoulder and armhole markings that were on your body when your measurements were taken (pic 10-1). Change the tissue shoulder until it matches your shoulder.

Back bodice and darts

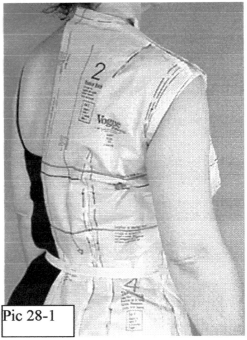
Pic 28-1

Back: *Linda has a flat, erect back. The large back dart was let out to reduce the shaping for a shoulder blade (Pic 28-1). The shoulder dart fits her shoulder.*

Armhole The armhole seam line must lie where the arm attaches to the body in the front and back (Pic 29-1). Mark any necessary changes on the tissue or make notes of what changes need to be made. The armhole of the tissue can easily be raised to increase mobility.

Neckline: Is the neckline of the tissue lying on your neckline? Mark any needed change on neckline of the pattern with a pencil or pins (Pic 27-1, 28-1 & 29-1).

Shoulder and armhole

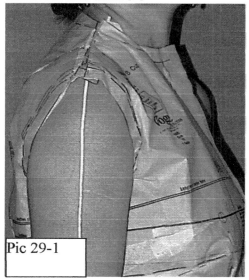

Pic 29-1

If you raise the armhole of the bodice front and back, the armhole of the sleeve must also be raised. If it is too high at the muslin pin fitting, the seam can be lowered and cut away. If it is not high enough you may need to cut a new bodice.

Sleeve: Slip on the sleeve and pin it to the bodice at match points in the front and back (Pic 30-1). The big dot on the sleeve is pinned to the shoulder seam. The small dots on the sleeve cap are pinned to the corresponding marks on the front and back bodice. Does the cross grain marked on the sleeve cap lie parallel to the floor? If it does not, reposition the sleeve until the cross grain is parallel and remark the match points and the dot marking the shoulder junction on the sleeve cap.

If needed, change the position of the underarm seam by adding to one side and removing seam from the other side so that the sleeve seam and the underarm match. If the change in sleeve cap is significant, check the measurement of the armhole and the sleeve cap. The sleeve cap, from underarm

to underarm, should be 1 to 1 ½ inches larger than the armhole.

Sleeve pinned into armhole.

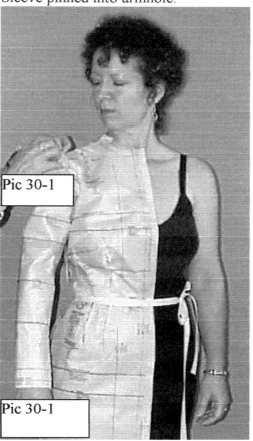

Pic 30-1

Pic 30-1

The elbow dart must be at the elbow and the sleeve should end at the wrist bone when the arm is bent (Pic 31-1). Bend your arm to check the elbow shaping and the length of the sleeve.

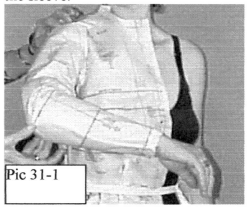

Pic 31-1

The sleeve should fit comfortably around the arm.

Skirt: The darts on the front and back of the skirt should end at the fullest part of the body and fit your body curves (Pic 32-1 & 33-1).

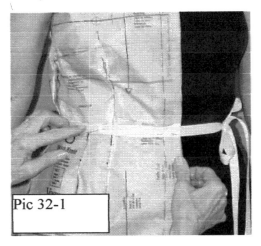

Pic 32-1

Back skirt darts

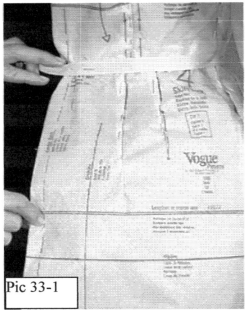

Pic 33-1

The skirt darts must give enough room for the body curves and end slightly above the fullest part of the body. Change the dart shaping when needed (Pic 32-1). The darts need to be shortened and the dart legs should be concave to give more room for the tummy curve. The center back dart is lengthened. The hip dart is shortened with concave legs to give room for the hip curve (Pic 33-1).

Tissue front
The pattern should come to your center front and center back (Pic 32-1, 33-1, 34-1). If it doesn't, let out the side seams. The seams should hang plumb. Put the plumb line belt

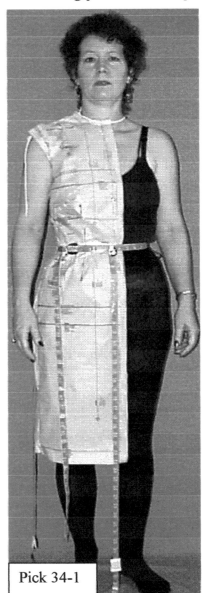

Pick 34-1

on the waistline to check the hang of the skirt at the side and at center front and back. If the seams are not hanging plumb with the plumb line lines on the plumb line belt adjust them at the waistline (pic 34-1).

Check the length of the skirt.

Take off the tissue and do any adjustments needed.

Try on the tissue and check the fit until you are satisfied the tissue is adjusted to fit your body and is hanging plumb.

You are ready to make up the pattern in muslin. Take the pattern apart and press the tissue. In Chapter 3 follow the directions in the segment titled "Marking and Sewing the Fitting Muslin."

Pin fit the Basic Dress Muslin

Fit is very personal. Some people like a snug fit, other like their garment looser. The fitting dress should be snug but not tight. It has only wearing ease. Wearing ease is room to shrug the shoulders without pulling the waistline of the dress from your waistline. You must be able to move your arms to the front (Pic 39-1) and to the back (Pic 38-1). The skirt should not cup the derriere (Pic 35-1 & 41-1). This close fit helps point out any fitting changes that may need adjustment in fashion garments. You probably would not want to wear a garment that was fit this closely unless it was a knit.

Linda wanted her dress with as much ease as possible.

Pic 35-1

Put the muslin on with the underclothing you wore for the tissue fit and that you will wear with your clothing. Pin the center front seam. Put on the plumb line belt.

Evaluate the following points following the sequence that was used on your basic as is listed below.

Bodice Length: The waistline of the dress should be at your waist. When the plumb line belt is on, the waistline should be under the belt.

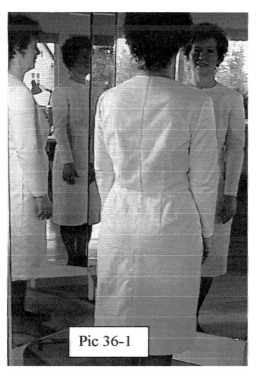

Pic 36-1

Bustline: The bodice should fit nicely over the bust with the darts ending ½ to 1 inch from the bust point with no fullness at the end of the dart (Pic 37-1 & 38-1).

Linda's bust line was increased to a C cup and her bust darts were lowered.

Shoulders seam: The shoulder seam should lie exactly at the top of the shoulder and end at the shoulder joint (Pic 37-1). It is easiest to check for the position of the shoulder joint before the sleeve is attached.

Linda's shoulder seam has been moved forward.

The sleeve should hang with the cross grain lines parallel to the floor (Pic 37-1). A pull at the top of the sleeve indicates a short sleeve cap. Be sure there is adequate sleeve cap at the shoulder.

Shoulder and sleeve

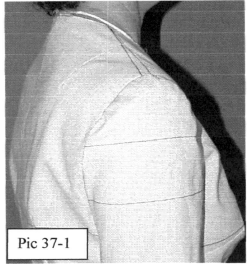

Pic 37-1

Front reach room

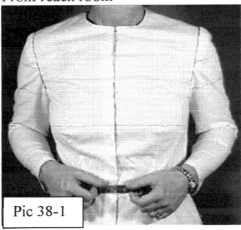

Pic 38-1

There should be adequate room to straighten the shoulders and move the elbows backward (Pic 38-1). The bodice should be snug but not tight.

Bodice back: The bodice back should fit nicely over the shoulders, with enough room to reach forward and cross your arms in the front. (Pick 39-1)

Linda's back waist dart was decreased because of her flat erect back.

Back reach room

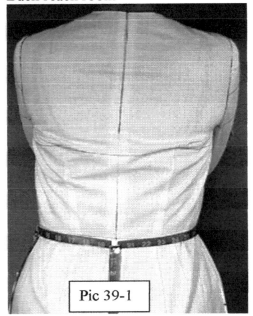

Pic 39-1

Armhole: The armhole seam must fit the body in the front and back. A high armhole in a close fitting garment gives more room for movement (Pic 38-1 & 39-1).

Linda's armhole was raised to reflect her armhole measurements and to give her ease of movement in a close fitted garment.

Neckline: A jewel neckline should lie at the base of the collarbone in front and at the prominent bone (top of spine) in the back. It should feel comfortable and lie flat (Pic 36-1, 37-1 & 40-1).

Sleeve: The sleeve should fit the armhole with adequate ease in the cap to allow for comfortable movement of the arm. There should be about one and one half inches ease in the sleeve at the biceps and enough room in the forearm to easily bend the arm (pic 40-1)

The cross grain marked on the cap should be parallel to the floor (Pic 37-1). The elbow dart should be at the elbow. The sleeve should end just below the bone at the wrist with a bent elbow (Pic 40-1).

Linda's sleeve must be lengthened above the elbow. Her elbow dart is slightly above her elbow. The change was made on her tissue after the muslin pin fitting.

Sleeve length and width

Pic 40-1

Waist and side seams

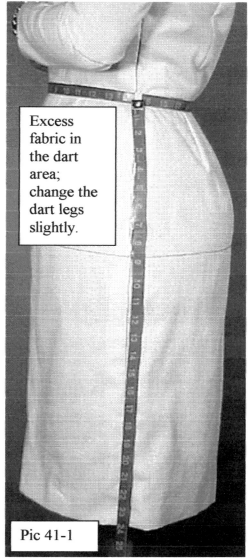

Excess fabric in the dart area; change the dart legs slightly.

Pic 41-1

Waist seam: The waist seam of the bodice front and back should be in the middle of the belt (Pic 41-1) with adequate room to shrug the shoulders.

Linda's waist seam was increased and her darts were changed to fit her body curves

Side seams: The bodice and skirt side seams should divide the body at the mid point of the armhole and hang plumb to the waistline. The plumb line belts at the side seams should be seen on the profile (Pic 39-1 Left side).

Linda has a flat area on her hips. The side seam was taken in between the three and seven inch hip line at the pin fitting (Pic 41-1).

Skirt: The skirt is eased onto the bodice. It must fit the hip at three, seven and nine inches from the waistline. The darts must end at the fullest part of the tummy curve in the front and the hip curve at the back. The large back dart allows room for the derriere. The side seams fit smoothly over the hip and divide the body at mid point hanging plumb from the armhole.

Linda's back dart legs will be straightened or curved outward to remove excess fabric above the 3 inch hip line.

51

Check all skirt seams with the plumb line belt.

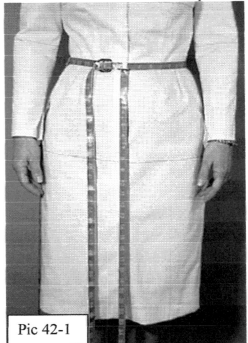

Pic 42-1

All skirt seams should hang plumb (sk 42-1). If there are irregularities in the hip height, a full tummy or a sway back remove the skirt from the bodice, adjust the waist line under the belt until all the seams are hanging plumb, remark the waist seam at the bottom of the belt and reattach the skirt. Occasionally some change also must be made to the bodice waist seam.

Skirt length: The fitting dress hem should be at a flattering place at the knee.

After all the adjustments are done to your satisfaction, correct any changes on the muslin and mark the entire pin fitting changes on the tissue.

Mark the date and your weight on the muslin and hang the completed garment in your closet.

The perfected tissue is your guide when adjusting fashion patterns.

The perfected muslin is your guide to check for any changes in your body. Each time you are beginning a new project try the muslin on and make sure it's still a perfect fit.

You are now ready to choose and adjust fashion patterns and sew beautiful clothing that fits.

Linda in her completed basic dress

Example 2: Linda's Basic Pattern and Fashion Pattern

Linda is a triangular figure type. She is 5 foot 2 inches tall, with a long waist for her height.

Comparing her measurements to the Industry Standard Measurement Chart, we found that Linda is a combination size measuring a size 6 in the shoulder, a size 10 in the high bust, front width and bodice length, a 12-14 in the waist and slightly larger than a 14 area in her hip.

Since the fit in the shoulder, high bust and front width are most important we chose a size 10 pattern for Linda

She does not want her garments tight so the pattern was adjusted with 3 inches of ease in the bust, 1-½ inches ease in the waist and 2 inches ease in the hip.

Her bust line is low and she wears a C cup bra.

She has a very flat, erect back and slightly forward shoulders.

To facilitate adjustment, we copied the flat tissue measurements of the basic pattern in size 10 from the Industry Standard Chart to her dress measurement chart in the spaces provided.

Begin by checking the bodice length, then check the bust line in this sequence before changing the pattern: Full bust, bust cup, bust tip, front width, front shoulder, and waist.

Back & front bodice length. Her back bodice measures slightly longer than the pattern and her front slightly shorter. No change is needed for the bodice length. The adjustment for the C cup will lengthen the front bodice. The bodice back length will be checked at the tissue fitting.

Full bust: Linda's full bust with 3 inches ease is 37 ½ inches. The pattern is 35 ¾ inches.

Bust Cup: Adding ¾ inch for the C cup gives us 36 ½ inches, still short one inch for her full bust measurement. Add the extra inch on the side seam of the front and back at the bust line. Divide the inch by four while working with a full pattern, which gives us an addition of ¼ inch on the side seams at the bust line of the front and back bodice.

Bust tip: Linda bust tip width is the same as the pattern, no change.

Front width: Her front width is 6 ¾ inches and the pattern is 7 inches. The shoulder

adjustment will make it slightly narrower. Check this again at the muslin pin fit.

Shoulder: Her shoulder is 4 ½ inches, the pattern is 4 ¾ inches. Decrease the shoulder ¼ inch on the bodice front. That will slightly decrease the front width.

Waist: Linda's waist is 26 ½ plus 1 ½ inches ease equals 28 inches. The pattern is 26 inches. Add 2 inches to the waist or ½ inch to the back and front.

Bust line placement: Linda's bust line is 14 ½ inches from the center back. The pattern is 13 ¼ . Her bust line is 1 ¼ inch lower than the pattern.

Linda's **front waistline** is 20 ¾ inches from the center back. The pattern measures 20 1/8 inches. Her waistline is 5/8 inch lower than the pattern.

Linda's measurement chart follows and then all the bust line and bodice front adjustments are done at once as shown on sketch 55-1.

EXAMPLE 2: Linda's Measurement Chart

Personal Body Measurements: Name: _Linda_____

Date:__10/28/99__   Pattern size:_10___   Height 5 ft 2 inches

Flat Pattern Measurement Chart **BODICE WIDTHS**

1. _32 1/2___   **1.** High Bust _32 ½_

2.__35 3/4___   **2.** Full Bust _**34 ½**_plus 2-3 inches ease_ **37 ½_ 2a.**Under Bust _28_

                           2a. Bra size _**34 C**_cup

3. _3 1/2____   **3.** Bust Tip Width_7__1/2 of total = bust dart placement on tissue __3 1/2___

4.__7_____   **4.** Front Width_13_ 1/2 = 6 1/2+ ¼ inches ease =__6 3/4_

                           4a. Distance from center front neckline to the front width _**4**_

5.__4 3/4____   **5.**Shoulder width R _4 1/2 L _4 1/2_ plus 1/8-1/4 equals back shoulder width _____

6.__7 5/8 +_   **6.** Back width _14 3/4_1/2 = _7 3/8_ + 3/8 inch ease_ 7 3/4_

                           6a. Distance from CB neckline __**7 3/8**__

7.__16 plus   **7.** Armhole depth (Measure with a weighted string)_15 ½ _

7a _**8**_____   7a. Front armhole to crease _*4 5/8*_

7b. _**6**_____   7b. Back armhole to crease_5 ½ _

7c.F_2 3/8__   **7c.** Underarm _5 3/8_____
  B _2_

8.__14 ¾ +_   **8.** Neckline _15 3/8____(measure with weighted string

8a._4 1/4_   **8a.** Front neckline _8 5/8 _____½ of front neckline __4 ¼ plus__

8b. _2 7/8 plus   **8b**. Back neckline __6 3/4 ___ ½ of back neckline __3 3/8_____

                          BODICE LENGTHS
9.__13 1/4___   **9.** Bust tip 15_____

9a.__20 1/8__   **9a.** Waistline (center back over bust tip to waist) _20 3/4_ and on to b, c, d, e, & f

                         9b. Blouse length _27 3/4___ **9c.** Bermuda length _37_____ **9d.** Knee length ___45_____

                         9e Long length __51 1/2___ **9f.** .Floor length __59_____

                         Flattering Lengths On Fashion Garments
                         Subtract waistline length 9a. 9c, 9d, 9e, & 9f.

                         9c. Bermuda length __16 1/4__   **89** Knee length __24 1/4____

9e. Long length _30 3/4___   8f. Floor length __38 1/4_____

10.__14 3/8__   10.Center front bodice length __14 1/2____

11.__16 1/4_   11.Center back bodice length ___16_____

12. __7 7/8_   12Side seam length __8 3/4____

SHOULDER SLOPE
13.__17____   13. Front slope R_161/2____L__16 3/4

14.___16 5/8_   14. Back slope R__17 ¼ __ L__17 ½__

ARM LENGTHS
15. _23 1/4__   15. Outside arm length _21 1/4____

15a._13 5/8_   15a. Shoulder to elbow __12 _____

15b._9 1/2__   15b. Elbow to wrist ___9 1/4____

ARM WIDTHS
16. __12 1/4   16. Fullest arm _11___+ 1 1/2" __12 1/2__ **16a.** distance from shoulder line __5 1/2__

16b._10 5/8_   **16b.** forearm._10 1/4__   **16c.**wrist _5 7/8__ **16d.** hand __8 3/4___

SKIRT MEASUREMENTS

Waist Line Adjustments: Length from waist to floor
17   17. Center back _39 1/4_____Left side __39 3/8_____

                 Center front __39_____Right side _39 3/8_____

SKIRT WIDTHS

WAIST & HIP MEASUREMENTS⊗ (Take with a plumb line belt)
18.__26____   **18.** Waist __26 ½__ +1-1 1/2" ease __28_____ = waistband length __28_____width___1 1/4___

19__33____   **19.** 3 inches from waist __35 1/2_+ 1-1 ¼ inches ease _36 ¾_

20. _36 1/4__   **20.** 7 inches from waist __38 3/4__ + 1 3/4- 2 inches ease _40 1/2___

21._36 1/4__   **21.** 9" from waist _39_____ + 2-3 inches ease __41_____

                 21a. Hip at the largest _39_____ Distance from waistline ___9_____inches

                 21b. Tape just slips off hip line- shows minimum amount of ease in a close fitted skirt__41_____

The bodice front is lengthened 5/8 inch, the bust is increased to a C cup and lowered 1 ¼ inches, the shoulder is narrowed ¼ inch, the full bust increased ¼ inch and waist line is increased ½ inch. The bust dart will automatically increase with the alteration for the C cup.

bodice and ¼ inch at the full bust on the back bodice.

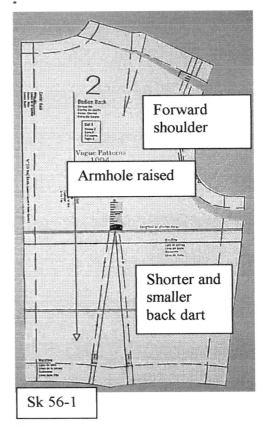

Forward shoulder

Armhole raised

Shorter and smaller back dart

Sk 56-1

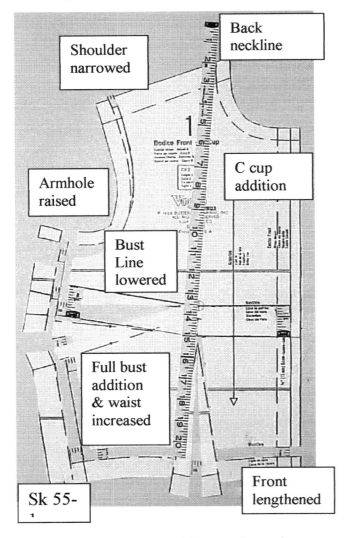

Shoulder narrowed

Back neckline

Armhole raised

C cup addition

Bust Line lowered

Full bust addition & waist increased

Front lengthened

Sk 55-1

Shoulder: The back shoulder remains a size 10 and is eased into the narrowed front shoulder. Linda has a forward shoulder. Add 3/8 inch to the shoulder at the armhole (sk 56-1)

Back width: Linda has a very erect flat back. Reduce the back bodice dart in width and length to remove back fullness and to add the ½ inch she needs in the waist on the back

Sleeve
Linda's sleeve length is 21 ¼ inches. She is 12 inches from shoulder to elbow and 9 ¼ inches from elbow to wrist.
The pattern is 23 ¼ inches. 13 5/8 inches from shoulder to elbow and 9 ½ inches from elbow to wrist.

The pattern was shortened 1 5/8 inches above the elbow and ¼ inch below the elbow. At the muslin pin fitting the sleeve was about 3/8 inch too short from the elbow to the shoulder. I readjusted the sleeve pattern to 1 ¼ inches and made a note on the muslin that the tissue was the correct length.

* Courtesy of Vogue Patterns, Butterick Co., 161 Avenue of the Americas, NY. NY 10013

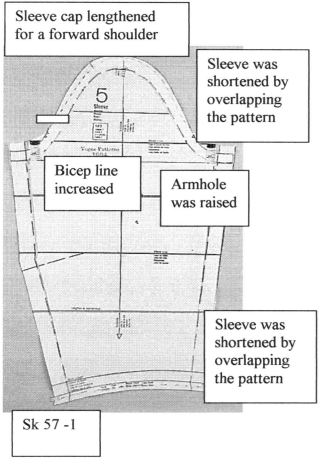

Sleeve cap lengthened for a forward shoulder

Sleeve was shortened by overlapping the pattern

Bicep line increased

Armhole was raised

Sleeve was shortened by overlapping the pattern

Sk 57 -1

The sleeve at the underarm or biceps line is 12 ¼ inches wide. Linda's full arm plus 1 ½ inches ease is 12 ½ inches. Since the bodice was increased ¼ inch on the front side seam add ¼ inch equally to the sleeve seams at the underarm.

Her armhole at the shoulder was altered for a forward shoulder. Alter the sleeve by lengthening the back sleeve cap 3/8 inch highlighted on picture by a bar (sk 57-1) that also raised the cap 3/8 inch. The adjustment is a little hard to see on the sketch because it was first lowered to shorten the sleeve 1 ¼ inches in length and then raised 3/8 inch for the forward shoulder adjustment.

The armhole on both the bodice and the sleeve was raised ½ inch to ensure enough height in the armhole (sk 55-1, 56-1 & 57-1). If it is too high at the pin fitting, lower it and trim off the excess fabric.

Skirt: Her length from waist to floor is ¼ inch longer at the center back. Increase the skirt ¼ inch at center back and raise the center back waist seam ¼ inch to adjust the back pattern to Linda's curves (sk 58-1).

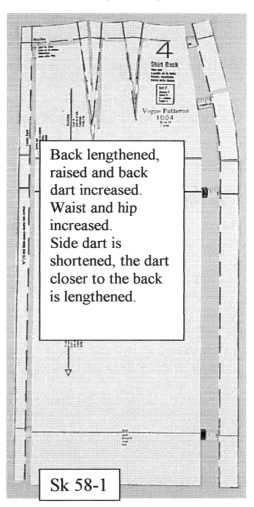

Back lengthened, raised and back dart increased. Waist and hip increased. Side dart is shortened, the dart closer to the back is lengthened.

Sk 58-1

The skirt front darts and the back hip dart were shortened and the legs of the darts were curved inward (concave) to give more room for her tummy and hip (sk 58-1 & 59-1). The derriere dart was increased and lengthened to provide more room (sk 58-1).

Skirt additions: (sk 58-1 & 59-1)
The skirt waistline must be slightly larger (1/2 inch) than the bodice. Increase the skirt at the

* Courtesy of Vogue Patterns, Butterick Co., 161 Avenue of the Americas, NY, NY 10013

side seams at total of 2 ½ inches or 5/8 inch on the back and front side seams.

Waist	5/8 inch
3 inches from waist	7/8 inch
7 inches from waist	1 inch
9" from waist	1 1/8 inch
Hip at the largest	must be a minimum of 41

Length of skirt:	Knee length 24 ¼
	Long length 30 ¾
	Floor length 38 ¼

The basic skirt was cut on the pattern line and hemmed with a 1 ½ inch hem.

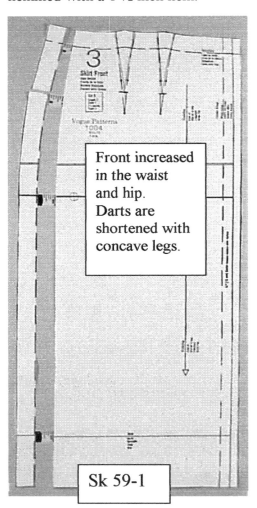

Front increased in the waist and hip. Darts are shortened with concave legs.

Sk 59-1

Linda's basic dress is done! She is ready to sew a real dress!

The dress is described on the envelope as a semi-fitted, lined straight dress, below mid-knee or above ankle, has shoulder pads, above elbow sleeves, mock wrap skirt, front overlay extending into right, tuck/concealed slit and back zipper.

For more information on Fashion Patterns refer to Part 11 Chapter 4: Choosing and Evaluating Fashion Patterns and Adjusting Fashion patterns

The flat tissue measure on the size 10 tissue pattern was:

Bust: 37 ¼ inches minus pattern envelope 32 ½ equals 5 inches of ease. Three inches is Linda's wearing ease. Two inches is design ease. Changing the bust cup size to Linda's C cup will give adequate ease in the bodice.

---

* Courtesy of Vogue Patterns, Butterick Co., 161 Avenue of the Americas, NY. NY 10013

Waist 29 ¼ inches minus the pattern envelope 25 equals 4 ¼ inches ease. Linda's waist plus ease is 28 inches. Add one inch to the waist.

Hip: 38 inches minus the pattern envelope 34 ½ inches equals 3 ½ inches ease. That is two inches of wearing ease and 1 ½ inches of design ease. Adding 1 inch at the 9 inch hip will give Linda an easy straight skirt.

The changes to the semi fitted fashion pattern are very similar to the basic tissue Since a garment hangs from the shoulder and a skirt hangs from the waist, the shoulder and waistline adjustments are always done. Wearing and design ease govern the width adjustments in Fashion Patterns.

Front Bodice: The bust line was increased to a C cup. The addition was extended to increase the waistline. There was plenty of design ease for the full bust measure. The bust dart was lowered to reflect Linda's lower bust line. The shoulder was narrowed and the armhole was raised (sk 60-1). Linda discovered she liked a high armhole because of the freedom of movement.

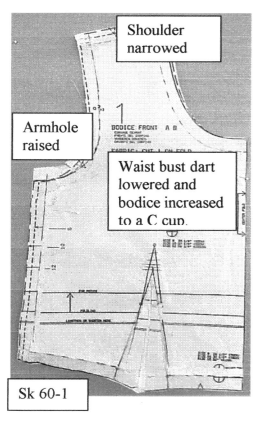

Shoulder narrowed

Armhole raised

Waist bust dart lowered and bodice increased to a C cup.

Sk 60-1

Back Bodice: The back bodice was altered for Linda's slightly forward shoulder. The back bodice dart was shortened and made smaller to fit her erect back which increased the back waistline (sk 61-1).

The back width was short of her basic measure by ¼ inch. The back width was increased in the armhole by ¼ inch (sk 61-1).

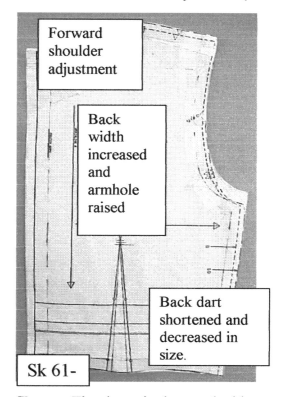

Forward shoulder adjustment

Back width increased and armhole raised

Back dart shortened and decreased in size.

Sk 61-

Sleeve: The sleeve is short and wide enough at the bicep line. The forward shoulder adjustment on the sleeve cap is marked by small bars (sk 62-1). We widened the back sleeve cap ¼ inch to correspond with the bodice back width adjustment (sk 61-1 & 62-1).

* Courtesy of Vogue Patterns, Butterick Co., 161 Avenue of the Americas, NY, NY 10013

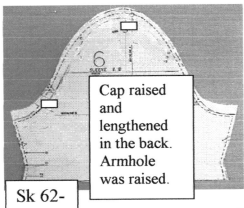

Cap raised and lengthened in the back. Armhole was raised.

Sk 62-

Skirt Front: One long dart will not fit Linda's front curves. The dart was changed from one long dart to two short darts (sk 63-1).

The pattern has a relaxed waistline designed to skim the body with 4 ¼ inches of ease in the waist. The skirt at the 9 inch hip is designed with 3 ½ inches of wearing and design ease: We increase the hip line by 1 inch at the 9 inch hip line.

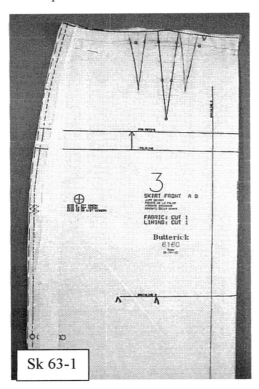

Sk 63-1

Skirt back: We increase the center back seam ¼ inch and raise the back waistline ¼ inch to give a total of 4 ½ inches of ease at the 9 inch hip line (sk 63-1 & 64-1). Linda likes her garments loose.

As a result of the relaxed waist line, the back skirt waistline, which was raised as the basic was raised (sk 58-1), was lowered at the pin fitting to make the center back seam hang plumb (sk 64-1).

The center back seam allowance on the skirt and back bodice were increased to 1 inch to accommodate a lapped zipper (sk 61-1 & 64-1).

Waistline was raised, then lowered after the pin fitting

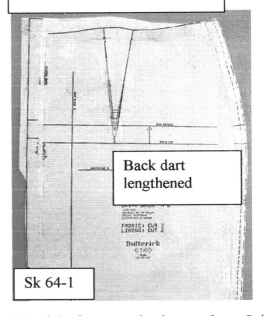

Back dart lengthened

Sk 64-1

The right front overlay has no darts. It is slightly eased in place of darts marked by a bar on the right front skirt (sk 65-1).

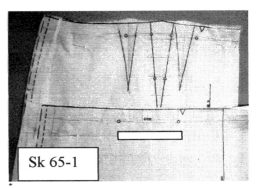

Sk 65-1

* Courtesy of Vogue Patterns, Butterick Co., 161 Avenue of the Americas, NY, NY 10013

The left front overlay was extended at the edge marked by a bar (sk 66-1) to match the increase in the hip line. [*]

Left front overlay has unstitched pleats that we shaped like darts to fit Linda's curves (sk 66-1).

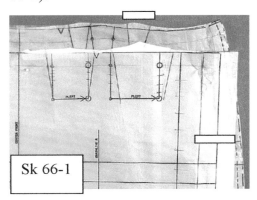

Sk 66-1

When the garment was being constructed, it was apparent the left front side dart marked by a bar (sk 66-1) must be changed to gathers instead of a stitched dart. The overlay on the right front was slightly gathered and it looked better for the skirt to be the same on both sides.

The skirt was pinned at 30 ½ inches from the waistline.

Linda's dress was made of her hand dyed silk Noil and lined with China silk.

Linda in her basic muslin holding her fashion pattern tissue.

Linda in her completed dress that fits!

[*] Courtesy of Vogue Patterns, Butterick Co., 161 Avenue of the Americas, NY, NY 10013

Chapter 2

Shirley in wool pants suit using Vogue 2946 View C for the slacks

Pant Measurement Chart

Personal Body Measurements: Name: _____ Date: _____

Pattern size: _____ Weight _____

You must have someone take your measurements.

Choose your pattern size by your snug 9 inch hip measurement. If using 1003 and you are between sizes choose the larger size. If using 2946 and you are between sizes choose the smaller size.

Flat Pattern Measurement	**Take or Copy these measurements from the Dress Measurement Chart**
	Waist & Hip Measurements⊗ (Take with a plumb line belt)
1._____	**1.** Waist _____ snug, but relax, breathe, add 1 - 2 inches ease _____ for waistband length
1a. _____	**1a**. Waistband length _____ width_____ . ½ of the waistband _____
1b. _____	**1b.** Waist seam _____. ½ of the waist seam _____
2. _____	**2.** 3 inches from waist _____ + 1-1 ¼ inches ease _____
3. _____	**3.** 7 inches from waist _____ + 1 3/4- 2 inches ease _____
4. _____	**4.** 9 inches from waist _____ + 2-3 inches ease _____
	4a. Hip at the largest _____ Distance from waistline _____ inches
	4b. Tape just slips off hip line- shows minimum amount of ease in a close fitted slack_____

ADDITIONAL MEASUREMENTS FOR SLACKS

Take sitting on a flat surface.

5. _____	**5.** Largest thigh _____ mark the leg then note the distance from the waist when standing _____
6. F_____	**6.** Crotch depth _____ from waist to the flat surface 1-2 inches ease _____

Take standing

7 ._____	**7.** Total crotch length from center front to center back _____
7a _____	**7a**. Front crotch length _____ Front curve_____
7b._____	**7b.** Back crotch length __ _____ Back Curve _____
	7c. Under crotch _____
8. _____	**8**. Waist to floor_____
8a.	**8a**. Waist to knee _____
9.	**9. Waistline adjustments: Length from waist to floor**

Center back _____ Left side _____

Center front _____ Right side _____

Taking Accurate Pant Measurements

Once your basic pants pattern is completed, use it when you are making pants. It can be worn for a fitted, slim leg pants. Your basic pants can also be used to adjust other pants but it is more accurate to make variations of your pattern.

Equipment Needed:
- Pants Measurement Chart (in this workbook)
- A Plumb line Kit: By the Sewing Arts®, Inc.

Some one to take the measurements: <u>You cannot take your own measurements. You cannot pin fit your own muslin.</u> If you do not have a sewing friend to assist you, hire a dressmaker to do the fitting for you. Make sure your helper follows directions, takes accurate measurements and gets all the information for you.

Locating body landmarks are essential when taking accurate measurements. Those landmarks are:

Waistline: Bend from side to side and make sure the plumb line belt is at your waist.

Spine: The spine at the waistline is center back. The tummy button at the waistline is center front.

Side seam: Arrange the plumb lines on the profile of your hip.

Take measurements over the undergarments (panties or panty hose) that you wear with most pants. Pants are usually fitted without support garments. Panty hose and especially support garments make the crotch measurement longer than just panties.

Prepare for the measurements:
- Place the belt (from the plumb line kit) snugly around the waistline (pic 1-2)
- Remove your shoes

Measurements are without ease! (No finger under the tape).

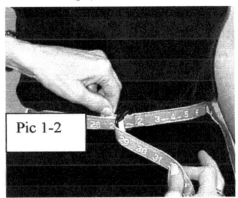

Pic 1-2

Use the plumb line belt to measure the waist.

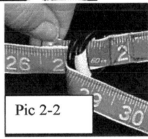

Pic 2-2

Numbers are from the Pant Measurement Chart
1.Waist: Snug but relax and breathe easy.

Hip Measurement
Measurement should be snug but not tight (pic 3-2).
The plumb line belt is used to keep the tape measure level on the body while the 3, 7, and 9-inch hip line are being measured. Picture 27-1 shows all the tapes on the hip for ease of photography.

Numbers are from the Pant Measurement Chart
2. Hip 3 inches from the waist: Measure with the tape even around the body (pic 3-2). This is usually the fullest part of the high hip. If the fullest part is lower measure that and note that it is lower than 3 inches.

Numbers are from the Pant Measurement Chart
3. Hip 7 inches from the waist: Measure with the tape even around the body (pic 3-2).

Numbers are from the Pant Measurement Chart

4. Hip 9 inches from the waist: Measure with the tape even around the body (pic 3-2).

Hip Measurements

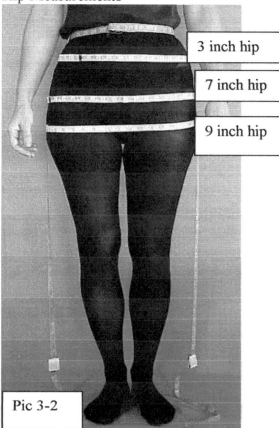

3 inch hip

7 inch hip

9 inch hip

Pic 3-2

Take sitting on a flat surface.

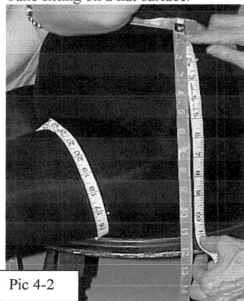

Pic 4-2

Numbers are from the Pant Measurement Chart

5. Thigh: Measure the largest part of the thigh. Mark the location on your leg (pic 4-2).

When you are standing (pic 9-2), measure the distance from the waist to the fullest part of your thigh.

Numbers are from the Pant Measurement Chart

6.Crotch Depth: Measure from the bottom of the belt over the hip curve to the flat surface (pic 4-2).

Take standing
Total crotch length and in-seam placement. Slip one plumb line off the belt. Put the belt on the waistline.

Crotch length and front and back crotch

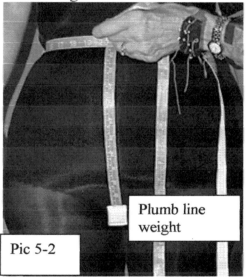

Plumb line weight

Pic 5-2

Place the plumb line tape measure between your legs with the stitched area of the weight in the front. Slip the ends of the tape measure under the belt at center front and back (pic 5-2).

Move the tape until the weight is just completely hidden at the front crotch and the tape is comfortable (not snug) under your body (pic 6-2).

Crotch length and front and back crotch

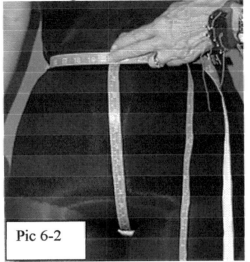

Pic 6-2

Mark the bottom of the belt on the plumb line tape with a pin or tape at center front and center back. This is the total crotch length (pic 6-2).

Numbers are from the Pant Measurement Chart
7. Total crotch length:
Measure from center back pin to center front pin for total crotch length (pic 30-1).

7a. Front crotch length:
Measure from the center front pin to the stitched edge of the weight for the front crotch length (pic 30-1).

Numbers are from the Pant Measurement Chart
7a. Front Curve:
Establish your front crotch curve by putting a tape between your legs. Hold the one-inch end at the bottom of the belt. Measure to the point the tape begins to go under the body (Pic 7-2).

7b. Back crotch length:
Measure from the center back pin to the stitched edge of the weight for the back crotch length (pic 6-2).

Numbers are from the Pant Measurement Chart
7b. Back curve:
Establish your back crotch curve by putting a tape between your legs. Hold the one-inch end at the bottom of the belt. Measure to the

point the tape begins to go under the body (Pic 32-1).

Crotch curves are used to adjust the crotch length.

Front curve

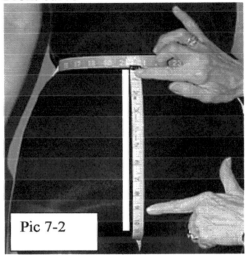

Pic 7-2

Back curve

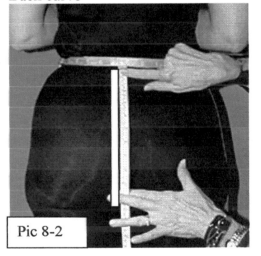

Pic 8-2

7c. Under crotch:
Subtract the front and back curves from the total crotch length to determine the length needed for the under crotch.

Numbers are from the Pant Measurement Chart
8. Waist to Floor:
Measure from bottom of the belt at the side seam to floor (pic 9-2). (No shoes)

8a. Waist to knee: Measure from bottom of the belt at the side seam to knee (pic 9-2).

Length to thigh, knee and floor

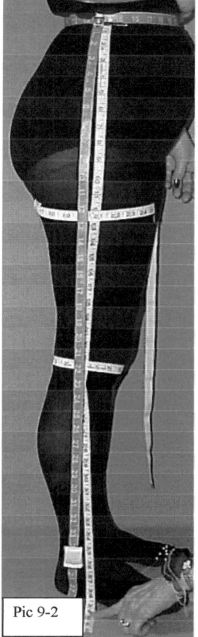

Pic 9-2

Numbers are from the Pant Measurement Chart

9. Waist Line Adjustments:
The person being measured should hold perfectly still. Move around the person you are measuring.

Slip the tape under the belt. Bring a one inch end of the tape to the floor. Note the measurement at the bottom of the belt marked with a bar (Pic 10-2).

Measure at:
Center front   Center back
Left side   Right side
These measurements indicate several figure differences that must be adjusted at the waistline such as high or large hip, sway back and a prominent tummy or derriere. They guide the pattern adjustment at the waistline.

Waist to floor length at centers and side seams

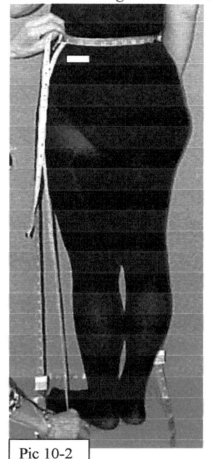

Pic 10-2

To choose your pattern size; compare your measurements in 9 inch hip area with the Industry Standard Pant Tissue Measurement Chart.

Adjust the basic slack pattern in the correct size using the measurements plus ease on the slack measurement chart.

It may be helpful to refer to Example 3: Linda's Basic Pant Pattern on pages 88 through 92.

Industry Standard Pant Tissue Measurement Chart

			6	8	10	12	
VOGUE 2946 & 1003 in size 6							
	Size		6	8	10	12	
	Pattern Envelope Waist		23	24	25	26 1/2	
	Pattern Envelope 9 inch hip		32 1/2	33 1/2	34 1/2	36	
	VOGUE 1003	size 6					
	1. Flat tissue waist		23 1/2	25 1/4	26 1/8	27 1/2	
	front		6	6 3/8	6 5/8	**7**	
	back		5 5/8	6 1/4	6 3/8 plus	6 3/4	
	half tissue		11 5/8	12 5/8	13 plus	13 3/4	
	1a. Waist band		**24 1/8**	**25**	**26**	**27 1/4**	
	1b. Half of waistband		12 plus	12 1/2	13	13 5/8	
WIDTHS	**2.** Hip 3" from waist		30 1/4	32 3/4	33 3/4	35 1/4	
	front		7 1/4	7 7/8	8 1/8	8 1/2	
	back		7 7/8	8 1/2	8 3/4	9 1/8	
	half tissue		15 1/8	16 3/8	16 7/8	17 5/8	
	3. Hip 7" from waist		35	36 1/2	37 1/2	39	
	front		8 1/8	8 1/2	8 3/4	9 1/8	
	back		9 3/8	9 3/4	10	10 3/8	
	half tissue		17 1/2	18 1/4	18 3/4	19 1/2	
	4. Hip 9" from waist		**36 1/4**	**37 3/8**	**38 1/2**	**39 3/4**	
	front		8 3/8	8 5/8	9	9 1/4	
	back		9 3/4	10	10 1/4	10 5/8	
	half tissue		18 1/8	18 5/8	19 1/4	19 7/8	
	5. Thigh		19 7/8	23 1/2	24 1/4	25	
	front thigh		9 1/4	9 7/8	10 1/4	10 5/8 plus	
	back thigh		11 5/8	13 5/8	14	14 1/4	
CROTCH	**6.** Front crotch depth		10 1/2	11	11 1/8	11 3/8 plus	
DEPTH	Back crotch depth		10 1/2	11 1/2	11 3/4	11 7/8 plus	
CROTCH	**6a.** Front crotch width		9 1/2	10	10 3/8	10 7/8	
WIDTH	Back crotch width		12	13 7/8	14 1/4	14 5/8	
LENGTH	**7.** Total crotch length		23 1/8	25 3/8	26	26 3/4	
	7a. Front crotch length		10 3/4	11 1/4	11 5/8	12 plus	
	7b. Back crotch length		12 3/8	14 1/8	14 3/8	14 5/8 plus	
SLACK	**8.** Waist to hem		37 1/2	40 1/2	40 1/2	40 1/2	
LENGTH							
LEG	Leg width at hem		11 7/8	12 1/2	13	13 1/2	
WIDTH	Front leg		5 3/8	5 1/2	5 3/4	6	
	Back leg		6 1/2	7	7 1/4	7 1/2	
If the measurement is 1/16 inch, it is shown as a plus or minus							

Courtesy of Vogue Patterns, Butterick Co., 161 Avenue of the Americas, NY, NY 10013

Industry Standard Pant Tissue Measurement Chart

VOGUE 2946 & 1003 in a size 14 (for comparsion)						
Size	14	14	16	18		
Pattern Envelope Waist	28	28	30	32		
Pattern Envelope 9 inch hip	38	38	40	42		
VOGUE 1003	**size 14**					
	Vogue 1003	Vogue 2946	Vogue 2946	Vogue 2946		
1. Flat tissue waist	29	29 3/4	31 3/4	33 3/4		
front	7 1/4	7 3/8	8	8 1/2		
back	7 1/4	7 3/8	7 7/8	8 3/8		
half tissue	14 1/2	14 7/8	15 7/8	16 7/8		
1a. Waist band	29		29	31	32 3/4	
1b. Half of waistband	14 1/2		14 1/2	15 1/2	16 3/8	
WIDTHS **2.** Hip 3" from waist	35 1/4	38 1/2	40 1/2	42 1/2		
front	8 1/2	9	9 1/2	10		
back	9 1/8	10 1/4	10 3/4	11 1/4		
half tissue	17 5/8	19 1/4	20 1/4	21 1/4		
3. Hip 7" from waist	40 1/4	41 3/4	43 1/4	45 1/4		
front	9 1/2	10 1/8	10 1/8	10 5/8		
back	10 5/8	11	11 1/2	12		
half tissue	20 1/8	22 1/8	21 5/8	22 5/8		
4. Hip 9" from waist	**41 1/2**	**42**	**43 7/8**	**45 7/8**		
front	9 3/4 minus	9 7/8	10 1/4	10 3/4		
back	113/4 minus	11 1/8 plus	11 5/8 plus	12 1/8 plus		
half tissue	20 3/4	21	21 7/8 plus	22 7/8 plus		
5. Thigh	24 1/8	26 1/2	27 5/8	28 7/8		
front thigh	11	11 3/8	12	12 5/8		
back thigh	13 1/8	15 1/8	15 5/8	16 1/4		
CROTCH **6.** Front crotch depth	11 1/2	11 3/4	11 7/8	12 1/8		
DEPTH Back crotch depth	11 5/8	12 1/4	12 1/2	12 7/8		
CROTCH **6a.** Front crotch width	11 3/8	11 1/2	12 1/8	12 3/4		
WIDTH Back crotch width	13 3/4	15 1/2	16 plus	16 5/8		
LENGTH **7.** Total crotch length	25 5/8	27 1/4	27 7/8	28 1/2		
7a. Front crotch length	11 7/8	12 3/8	12 5/8	13		
7b. Back crotch length	13 3/4	14 7/8	15 1/4	15 1/2		
SLACK **8.** Waist to hem	37 5/8	40 1/2	40 3/8	40 1/2		
LENGTH						
LEG Leg width at hem	13 3/4	14 1/8 plus	14 5/8	15 1/8 plus		
WIDTH Front leg	6 1/4	6 1/4 plus	6 1/2	6 3/4		
Back leg	7 1/2	7 7/8	8 1/8	8 3/8		
If the measurement is 1/16 inch, it is shown as a plus or minus						

Courtesy of Vogue Patterns, Butterick Co., 161 Avenue of the Americas, NY, NY 10013

Industry Standard Pant Tissue Measurement Chart

VOGUE 2946					
	Size		20	22	24
	Pattern Envelope Waist		34	37	39
	Pattern Envelope 9 inch hip		44	46	48
	1. Flat tissue waist		35 3/4	38 1/2	40 1/2
	front		9	9 3/4	10 1/4
	back		8 7/8	9 1/2	10
	half tissue		17 7/8	191/4	20 1/4
	1a. Waist band		34 3/4	37 7/8	39 3/4
	1b. Half of waistband		17 3/8	18 7/8	19 7/8
WIDTHS	**2.** Hip 3" from waist		43 1/2	46	47 3/4
	front		10 5/8	11 1/4	11 5/8
	back		11 1/8	11 3/4	12 1/4
	half tissue		21 3/4	23	23 7/8
	3. Hip 7" from waist		47	49 1/2	51 1/2
	front		11 1/8	11 3/4	12 1/4
	back		12 3/8 plus	13	13 1/2
	half tissue		23 1/2	24 3/4	25 3/4
	4. Hip 9" from waist		47 3/4	50	51 3/4
	front		11 1/4	11 3/4	12 1/4
	back		12 5/8	13 1/8	13 5/8
	half tissue		23 7/8	25	25 7/8
	5. Thigh		29 7/8	31	32 1/4
	front thigh		13 1/8	13 5/8	14 1/4
	back thigh		16 3/4 plus	17 3/8	18
CROTCH	**6.** Front crotch depth		12 1/2	12 3/4	13
DEPTH	Back crotch depth		13 inches	13 1/4	13 1/2
CROTCH	**6a.** Front crotch width		13 3/8	14	14 1/2
WIDTH	Back crotch width		17 1/4	17 7/8	18 3/8
LENGTH	**7.** Total crotch length		29 1/4	30 1/8	31
	7a. Front crotch length		13 3/8	14	14 1/2
	7b. Back crotch length		15 7/8	16 1/8	16 1/2
SLACK	**8.** Waist to hem		40 1/2	40 1/2	40 1/2
LENGTH					
LEG	Leg width at hem		15 3/4	16 1/8	16 5/8 plus
WIDTH	Front leg		7 1/8	7 3/8	7 5/8
	Back leg		8 5/8	8 3/4	9 plus
	If the measurement is 1/16 inch, it is shown as a plus or minus				

Courtesy of Vogue Patterns, Butterick Co., 161 Avenue of the Americas, NY, NY 10013

Adjusting the Basic Pant Pattern to Your Measurements

As with the dress pattern the goal when adjusting a pant pattern is to achieve a great fit with the fewest changes. **Choose your pant pattern size by a snug hip measurement nine inches from your waist**. I suggest **Vogue 1003** (the pant basic) or **Vogue basic design 2946 View E.** Vogue 1003 has only wearing ease allowed. Vogue 2946 has wearing and design ease allowed. If you are between sizes choose the larger size when using 1003 and the smaller size when using 2946. Check the Standard Flat Tissue Measurements in this book before you choose your pattern size.

I use Vogue 2946 when I am doing a pant fitting for a client because she can use the pleated versions for her fashion slacks by adjusting them in the same way I adjusted her basic. For detailed instructions on sewing pants after fitting, you should refer to "The Art Of Sewing Basics & Beyond.

Pants and skirt are fitted almost the same from the waist to the nine-inch hipline. If you have adjusted the basic dress pattern, you can use waistline, hipline and dart adjustments that were made on the skirt.

Like a skirt, a pant must hang with the side seams perpendicular to the floor and the cross grain lines parallel to the floor, however on a pant the center front and back seams end in the crotch making it a bit more difficult to adjust the hang of the pants.

Pants with a front opening should always have a center back seam in the waistband. Waistband width is usually 1¼ inch wide, however if you are curvy above and below the waistline use a narrow (3/4 -1 inch) wide waistband. If you have a long smooth torso, you can wear a wider (1 1/2-2 inch) waistband.
The width of the waistband influences the length of the band. A pants waistband should be longer than a skirt waistband. A looser waistband is more flattering if hips are ten inches or larger than the waistline. When you have determined how wide and how long your waistband will be, test it by placing the waistband interfacing around your waist. Sit and relax, making sure the waistband is comfortable.

Sequence of pattern adjustment
Numbers are from the pant measurement chart

Crotch Depth	6
Pant Length to Floor	8
Waistline Adjustments	9
Total Crotch Length	7
Waistband	1a
Waistline	1
Hip	2,3,4
Thigh	5

As you can see the numbers are not in order, however, the sequence is important for accuracy and ease of pattern adjustment.

Crotch Depth (6) Measure from the waistline along the side seam to the crotch line on the front pattern (sk 1-2).

Adjust both the back and front tissue.

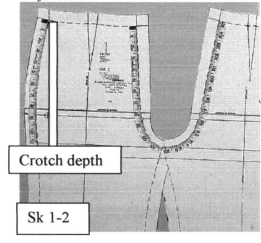

Crotch depth

Sk 1-2

Numbers are from the pants measurement chart.
6. Crotch depth (your measurement plus ease from your measurement chart _____
The pattern crotch depth (numbers are from the Industry Standard Pant Tissue measurements) _____Lengthen or shorten.

Shorten both the front and back crotch

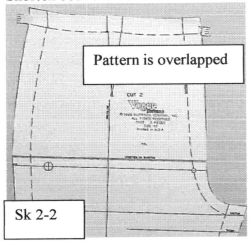

Pattern is overlapped

Sk 2-2

Lengthen both the front and back crotch (sk 2-2 & 3-2).

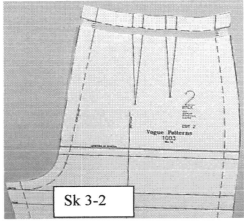

Sk 3-2

Wearing ease
Waistband: 1 1/2 – 2 inches larger than a snug waist measurement
Waistline: 1 inch larger than the waistband
Hip: 2-3 inches
Crotch: ½ -1 inch longer than crotch depth
Total crotch of pants must measure your total crotch measurement.

Numbers are from the pant measurement chart.
Pant Length (8
Measure the length from the waist to the floor at the side seam (sk 5-2). Without shoes.
Pant lengthened at the hemline (sk 5-2)
Allow two inches for a hem.

Extend the straight of grain (sk 4-2 & 5-2) before lengthening or shortening the pants leg.

Pant shortened

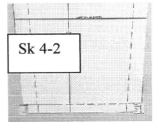

Sk 4-2

Pants shortened at the hemline by over-lapping the pattern (sk 4-2).

Pant Length and lengthening the leg

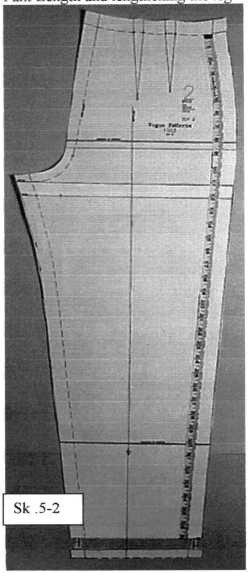

Sk .5-2

Waistline adjustments (9): The waistline adjustments must be made for posture, pelvic tilt and extra weight. These adjustments, made at the waistline seam, affect the pant widths at the waist and hipline. The low front waist adjustment affects the length measurements. When you do the adjustment for a low front waist; (sk 8-2) recheck the crotch depth (sk 1-2) and the length of the pants (sk 5-2).

Prominent Tummy
The front length measures longer than the back and the tummy on the profile is significant.

Numbers are from the slack measurement chart.
Length from waist to floor
9. Center back _____ Center front _____
Difference _____

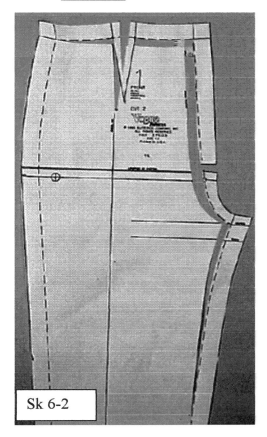

Sk 6-2

Raise the center front waistline seam (sk 6-2) the difference between center front and center back.
Extend the center front waistline and inseam the same amount (sk 6-2).

Prominent Derriere
The back length measures longer than the front length and the derriere on the profile is significant.

Length from waist to floor
9. Center back _____ Center front _____
Difference _____
Raise the center back waistline seam the difference between the front and back.

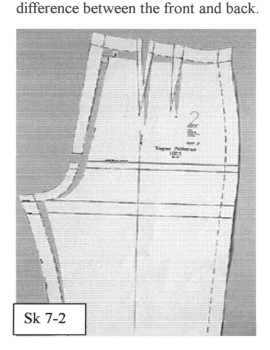

Sk 7-2

Extend the center back seam and inseam the same amount. Slash through the derriere dart and spread the dart to provide more shaping for the derriere (sk 7-2).

Low Front Waist
Pelvic tilt or weight gain has resulted in a low front waistline. The front of all garments are too long. The waist seam needs to be lowered at the center front.

Lowered front waist

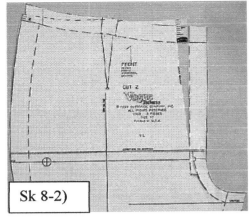

Sk 8-2)

The center front waist seam is lowered (sk 8-2). The center back waist seam is at the normal seam line. When the side seam is lowered, the front and back side seam must be lowered equally (sk 8-2 & 9-2). The crotch depth and pant length become shorter.

Back side seam is lowered to match the front side seam. The center back is unchanged (sk8-2 & 9-2).

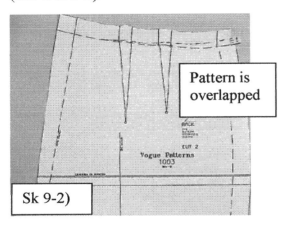

Pattern is overlapped

Sk 9-2)

Numbers are from the pant measurement chart.
Length from waist to floor
9. Center back _____ Center front _____
Difference _____

Tip: *Use caution when you lower a seam, it cannot be raised without adequate seam allowance*

Extend the original center front seam to the cutting line (sk 8-2). Allow extra seam

allowance for further adjustment at the pin fitting. It can easily be removed if necessary.

Low (sway) Back
The pelvic tilt or posture makes the back shorter than the front. This adjustment may present itself at the muslin pin fitting as a wrinkled area just below the waistband. Pin a tuck under the waistband removing the excess fabric. Remark the waist seam lowering the center back seam and tapering the waist seam to the original waist seam at the side seam (sk 10-2). Extend the original center back seam to the cutting line. Only the waist is lowered unless the derriere curve is also low (sk 14-2).

Numbers are from the pant measurement chart.
Length from waist to floor
9. Center back _____ Center front _____
Difference _____

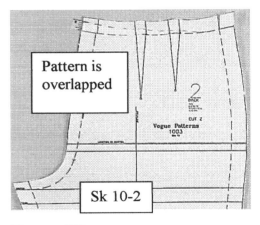

Pattern is overlapped

Sk 10-2

Uneven Hip
One hip measures longer from waist to floor than the other hip. The hip that is high is usually larger and will need more width at the hipline. The larger side may require a longer waistband due to the higher, larger hip.

Numbers are from the pant measurement chart.
Length from waist to floor
9. Left side _____ Right side _____
Difference _____

Tip! *Put Removable tape on the seam lines and mark the right side with a red pencil and the left side with a green pencil.*

The front and back seams are adjusted equally.
Uneven hip adjustment

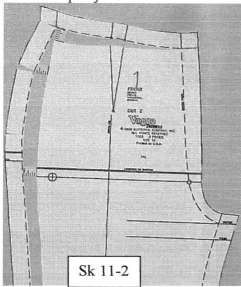

Sk 11-2

The pattern waist seam line (cut line) is the low side; the raised seam allowance is the high side (sk11-2 & 12-2).

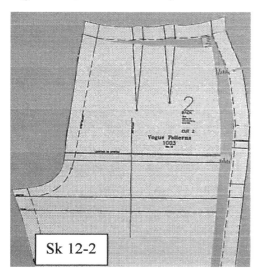

Sk 12-2

The waist and side seam are evaluated at the tissue fitting and perfected at the pin fitting. The goal is to have enough seam allowance at the waist and hip for the high large hip. After the pin fitting, permanently mark the tissue.

Total Crotch Length (7)

The crotch presents the challenge of balancing the length of the front crotch and back crotch and making the crotch curves fit your body. Adjustments are done at the crotch curve and the waistline using a plumb line belt to check the hang of the pants. The fit in the crotch is very individual and must be comfortable. The inseam should not be seen from the front or back of the pants.

The crotch seam is an under body seam (sk 13-2). Raising the crotch shortens the crotch seam. Lowering the crotch lengthens the crotch seam. If a crotch is too high, you can simply stitch it lower. If the crotch is too low, you must lower the waistband.

The crotch is divided into the front curve, marked on the pattern with a dot, the back curve, marked on the pattern with a dot and the front and back under body crotch.

Total crotch length
Front and Back Curves:

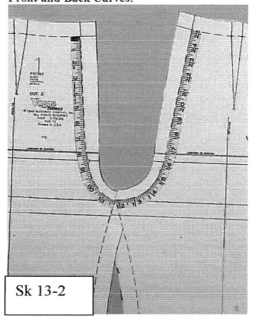

Sk 13-2

When you are adjusting for a prominent derriere or tummy, the curves will measure longer and should be adjusted at the center back and center front waistline seam (sk 7-2 & 6-2) . The exception is a low derriere, which requires that the back curve be deepened or lowered (sk 14-2). The back curve can be lowered to lengthen the back crotch only in the curve or it can be lowered at the waist seam line (sk 10-2).

Measure the pattern by turning the tape on edge to measure around the curve. Lengthen or shorten the total crotch according to your measurements.

Numbers are from the pant measurement chart.

7. Your crotch length from center front to center back

_____
7a. Front crotch length _____ front curve _____
7b. Back crotch length _____ back
curve_____

Tip: *The inseam at the back can be 3/8 inch shorter than the front inseam. Steam-stretch the back inseam; ease the front on the back to help eliminate the excess in the back of the pant just below the derriere (sk 14-2).*

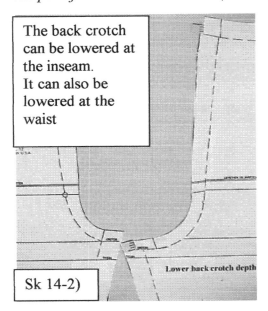

The back crotch can be lowered at the inseam.
It can also be lowered at the waist

Lower back crotch depth

Sk 14-2)

In-seam: The inseam is used to adjust the underbody segment of the crotch seam. Any adjustment on the inseam is easily changed at the tissue fitting or the pin fitting. Senior figures with a full waist, a tummy and a flat derriere may require more room at the front inseam and less at the back inseam.

Tip: *Allow extra one to one and a half inch seam allowance (sk 15-2 Senior Figure)*

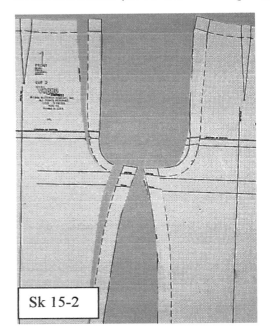

Sk 15-2

Waistband (1a)
The waistband measure for pants should be at least ½ longer than a skirt waistband. Be sure it is comfortable when you are sitting. The waistband for pants with a front opening always has a center back seam (sk 16-2).

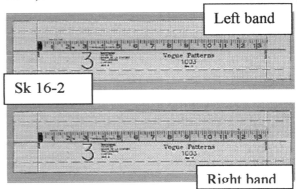

Left band

Sk 16-2

Right band

Numbers are from the pant measurement chart.
1. Waist _____ snug but breathe add 1 ½ to 2 inches **1a.** Waistband length _____ width_____

1b. ½ of the waistband_____

Pant Widths (2, 3, 4 & 5):
Mark the distance from the waist seam on the side seams at 3-7-9 inches from the waist and the thigh (sk 17-2 & 18-2). The pattern must be adjusted to your measurements plus

the wearing ease allowed. The tissue measurements are on the Pant Standard Tissue Measurements in each size.
The **waist seam** (sk 17-2 & 18-2) of the pants must be 1 inch larger than the **waistband** (sk 16-2). An accentuated hip curve requires more ease. Before adjusting the waistline measurement, evaluate the amount needed.

Numbers are from the pants measurement chart.
Waistband of pants plus 1-1½ inches equals the **waist seam (1b** on the measurement chart) of the pants_____.
One half of the waist seam is _____.
Waist seam (flat tissue measurement from chart) _____ difference (your waistline)_____ divide by 2 Add _____ to the waistline of your tissue, to achieve the adjusted measurement of your tissue waistline.

Waist seam adjustment is done at center front, center back, darts and the remainder at the side seams depending on your curves. The pants waist seam is eased onto the waistband.

Front waist, hip and thigh measurements

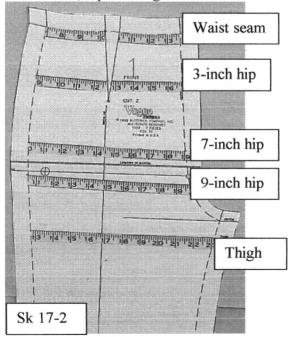

Sk 17-2

Back waist, hip and thigh measurements

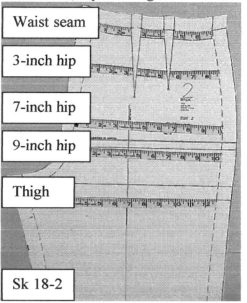

| Waist seam |
| 3-inch hip |
| 7-inch hip |
| 9-inch hip |
| Thigh |

Sk 18-2

Numbers are from the pants measurement chart.
2. 3 inches from waist (your measurement)_____plus ease _____ ½ _____.
Flat tissue measurement from chart _____ plus or minus _____Divide by two _____

Front waistline adjustment at seams and darts

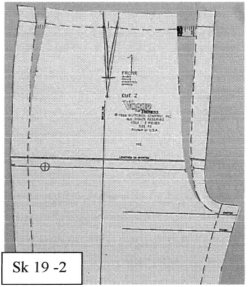

Sk 19 -2

Courtesy of Vogue Patterns, Butterick Co., 161 Avenue of the Americas, NY, NY 10013

Back waistline adjustment at seams and darts

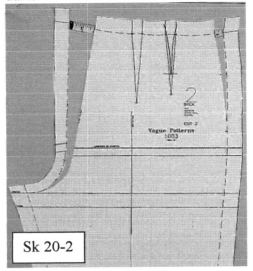

Sk 20-2

Waist adjustment at side seam and hip adjustment at side seams and crotch seams

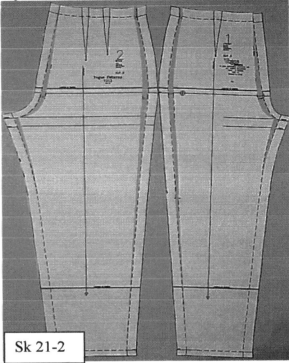

Sk 21-2

The waistline is adjusted at the side seams and the darts (sk 19-2 & 20-2). The front darts and the back side-dart should end at the high hip (sk 19-2 & 20-2). The high hip is the fullest part of the hip and stomach curve. Darts give fullness. If you aren't very rounded decrease the depth of the dart, especially if you need a larger waistline than the pattern has allowed. If you are very rounded and need more shape make the darts deeper or add another dart.

Numbers are from the pants measurement chart.
3. 7 inches from waist (your
measurement)_____plus ease _____ ½ _____
Flat tissue measurement from chart _____ plus or
minus _____Divide by two _____

Numbers are from the pants measurement chart.
4. 9 inches from waist (your
measurement)_____plus ease _____ ½ _____
Flat tissue measurement from chart _____ plus or
minus _____Divide by two _____

The hip may be larger below or above the nine-inch mark on the skirt.
Numbers are from the pants measurement chart.
4a. Hip at the largest ____Distance from
waistline___

Measurement from the pants measurement chart
4b. Tape slips off hip line _____

Additions to the hipline can vary from waist to hip. Blend the widened hip at the largest to the leg width at the hem. Additions are done evenly to the back and front pant on the side seam.
The front darts are shortened to end at the fullest curve of the tummy and the legs are curved inward (concave) to give more room over the rounded stomach (sk 18-2).

The back dart closest to the center back seam gives shape for the derriere. It can be adjusted in length and depth to fit the curve of the derriere. It must end at the fullest curve (sk 20-2). If the derriere is significant, the center back dart legs may be convex (curve out) to remove excess fabric below the waistline or the dart legs can be straight to provide shaping for the derriere. The back hip dart is shortened to end at the hip curve. The dart legs are curved inward to give more hip room (sk 20-2).

The shape and length of the darts must fit your curves. Review Adjusting Darts.

Add to the hip widths below the darts at the crotch and then to the side seam (sk 21-2). Your hip shape influences the addition. A very curved hip line requires adding to the side seam. A very flat hip line requires adding to the crotch seam.

Pin the tissue together and tissue fit one leg to check the length and width adjustments.

Courtesy of Vogue Patterns, Butterick Co., 161 Avenue of the Americas, NY, NY 10013

Tissue Fitting the Pants Basic Pattern

The tissue fitting is always a valuable way to check the pattern adjustments you have made without actually making up the pants in fabric. It involves pinning or taping the backed pattern pieces together, usually half a garment (Pic 14-2 & 15-2), trying it on, evaluating the fit and making any necessary changes until you are happy with the pattern. If your right and left sides are noticeably different make a full tissue and tissue fit the sides individually. Any needed changes are made on the tissue before cutting and sewing the fitting muslin.

Prepare the Pattern
Pin all the darts.

Reinforce the crotch seam with narrow strips of tape. Clip the curves and press the front and back crotch seam to the wrong side (pic 12-2 & 13-2.

On the front pattern, fold the inseam and side seam to the inside (pic 12-2). Fold the hem up and pin (pic 14-2).

Pin the front and back together along the inseam and side seams leaving a few inches free so you have room to get your foot through the pant leg (14-2).

Pinning the tissue seams

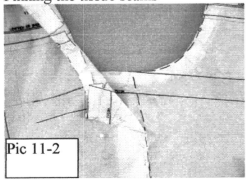

Pic 11-2

Tip: *Pin a narrow ribbon (long enough to go around your waist and tie together) to the waistline of the pattern.*

Pin a narrow ribbon long enough to go around your waist and tie together to the waistline of the pattern (pic 14-2).

Front leg

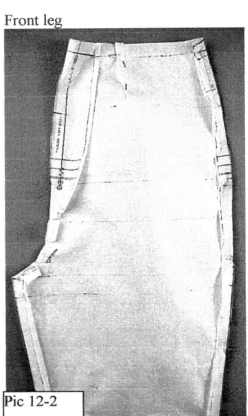

Pic 12-2

Back leg

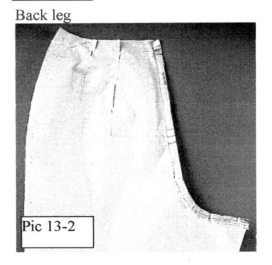

Pic 13-2

Tissue ready for the pin fitting

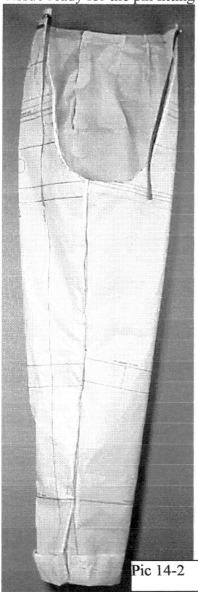

Pic 14-2

Prepare for tissue fitting the basic pants
Try the tissue on over the under garments
(support garment, panty hose, or panties)
that you wore when your measurements
were taken, without shoes.

Tissue fitting
Carefully slip the tissue on your body and tie
the ribbon around your waist (pic 15-2).

Evaluate Your Pattern
Cross grain lines and seam lines: The
basic fitting pant is closely fitted. The side
seam should hang perpendicular to the floor
and the cross grain lines should be parallel
to the floor. Check the side seam with the
plumb line belt (Pick 15-2). If it doesn't
hang straight, adjust the tissue at the
waistline on the pant until it hangs
perpendicular to the floor.

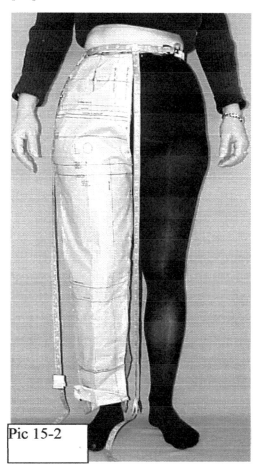

Pic 15-2

Side seam:
The side seam should divide the body where
the plumb line hangs on the hip profile (pic
15-2). If it does not, move the side seam so
that the seam is in the proper place on the
hip.

Waistline and center front seam:
The center front seam of the pattern should
come to your center front at the crotch seam
(pic 15-2 & 16-2). If it doesn't, let out the

crotch seam or the side seams. The inseam should not be seen from the front or the back.

Hipline: The tissue hip line should fit your hip with the darts giving shape for your curves. Linda's front dart was moved toward the center of her pattern and made shorter with curved inward (concave) dart legs. The side back dart was made shorter with concave legs. The derriere dart was lengthened.

Tissue back

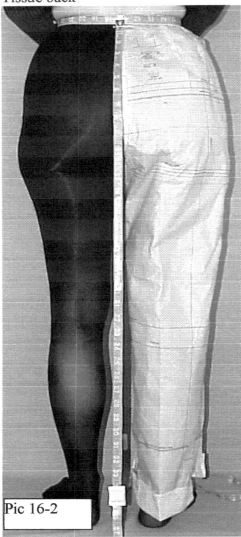

Pic 16-2

Crotch:
The pattern should come to your center back and front at the crotch seam. If it doesn't, let out the crotch seam or the side seams.

Linda's pattern was let out in both the front and back crotch.

Thigh: The thigh seems adequate except in the front where it was increased along with the crotch width.

Tissue side view

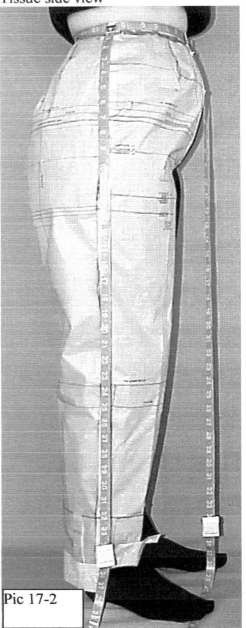

Pic 17-2

Pant length: Even though the front crotch length appears to be long, it is safer to correct the crotch lengths at the pin fitting. However, if the tissue is short in crotch or leg length it must be lengthened.

Check the fit until you are satisfied. When you are satisfied, take the pattern apart. Press the pattern and follow the directions in the chapter "Marking and Sewing the Fitting Muslin."

Pin fit the Basic Pant Muslin

Fit is the ultimate goal in sewing pants. The fitting pant should be comfortable for the wearer when she is walking and sitting as well as looking good when she is standing.

Linda's pattern was adjusted with wearing ease:
1 ½ inches ease in the waist
2 inches ease in the hips

A pleated version will have more room. This close, but wearable, fit helps point out any fitting changes that may need adjustment. The fitting pant can be constructed of any firm woven fabric with no stretch and can be worn as a slim pant.

Be very careful when fitting the crotch length. This underbody seam demands a balance between the front and the back that is unnecessary in any other part of a garment. The front crotch must be low enough to allow movement without feeling constrictive but high enough so that it does not look long or feel long when you walk. The back crotch must be long enough for you to walk and step up, as in going up stairs, without the pant pulling uncomfortably on the front thigh. Most of us want a perfectly smooth hanging back with no excess under the derriere, however there <u>must</u> be enough stride room (room in the back inseam and crotch) for you to move and sit comfortably.

Put the pant muslin on with the underclothing you wore for the tissue fit and that you will wear with your pants. Pin the center front seam and the waistband. Put on the plumb line belt.

First look: The pant is roomy enough and Linda says it is comfortable (pic 18-2) but when she steps the front crotch looks a bit long (pic 19-2) and the area under the back derriere is too loose (pic 20-2).

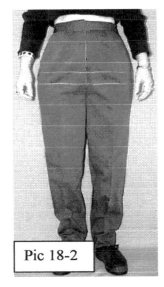

Pic 18-2

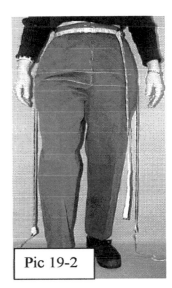

Pic 19-2

Pic 20-2

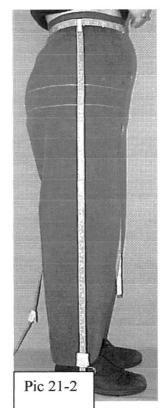

Pic 21-2

Roll up the hem so the pant is hanging without a break and check the following points in sequence.

Cross grain: The cross grain lines are parallel to the floor even though the crotch distorts the back cross grain slightly. The

84

grain lines are adjusted at the waistline if they are not parallel to the floor.

Side seams and front crease: The side seam divides the body and is hanging plumb with the belt (pic 21-2). The front creases are hanging plumb.

Waist: The waistline is comfortable but there should be more ease in the center front area. The front darts are too deep causing too much fullness (pic 22-2).

Hip: The hip line has adequate room. The side seam curve between 3 and 9 inches needs to be flattened slightly (pic 22-2 & 23-2). The back derriere dart needs to be moved closer to the center back seam and needs to be taken in to remove excess fabric above the derriere curve (pic 23-2).

Crotch: There is adequate room in the underbody seam but it looks as if we need more room in the front crotch curve (sk 15-2) and inseam and less in the back (pic 23-2 & 24-2).

Thigh: There is adequate room in the thigh but we need more room in the front and less in the back (pic 23-2 & 24-2).

Pant Length: The pant is almost too long for a slim leg (pic 18-2).

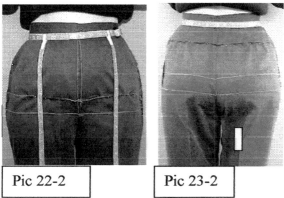

| Pic 22-2 | Pic 23-2 |

Adjustments at the Pin fitting:
- The front and back curves are shortened (pic 22-2 & 23-2).
- She needs a bit more room in the center front seam so the front was released (pic

22-2). The addition will extend into the front inseam.
- A tuck has been pinned in the back inseam marked by a bar in (pic 23-2).

The pants were taken off and the following adjustments were done:
The side seams were taken in 1/8 inch between the 3 and 9 inch hip line to straighten the hip curve (pic 22-2 and 23-2).

The **front** crotch curve at the inseam was raised ½ inch, the center front seam was increased ¼ inch, a total of ½ inch, at the 7 inch hip line and tapered to the center front at the waistline.

The **waistline** was lowered shortening the crotch ¼ inch at the center front, ¼ inch at the side seam and 5/8 inch at center back (pic 23-2).

The **back** inseam was taken in 5/8 inch at the crotch and tapered to the regular seam line 12 inches below the crotch (pic 25-2).

Re-evaluation: The pants are fitting much nicer but a few more adjustments will improve the fit.

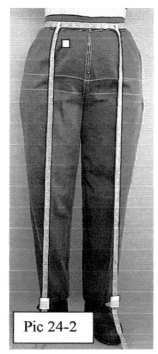

Pic 24-2

The front crotch curve is still ¼ inch too long and has been pinned up (pic 24-2). The front darts are too deep which cause excess fabric at the dart end marked by a white square (pic 24-2) and some ease is needed at the center front.

The front creases are hanging plumb.

The side seams are fitting Linda's curves and hanging

plumb but the pant is still not fitting nicely at the front crotch (pic 26-2). We need more room in the front inseam (pic 24-2).

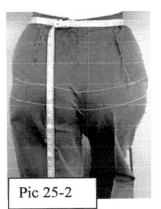

Pic 25-2

The back has some excess fabric in the dart area. We pinned the darts so the legs curved out (convex) to remove the excess fabric and still give room for the derriere curve (pic 25-2). The dart would fit better if it were closer to the center back seam.

Linda has adequate room in the back stride to comfortably take a step (pic-25-2).

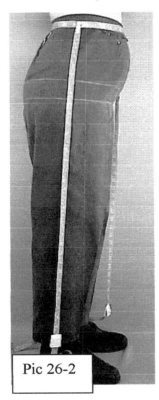

Pic 26-2

The pants were taken off and the following adjustments were done:

- The waistband was lowered another ¼ inch.

- The front darts were released 1/8 inch with the extra fabric eased into the waistband at the center front.
- The front inseam was let out ½ inch.
- The back derriere dart was moved toward the back seam ½ inch and the dart legs were made concave.

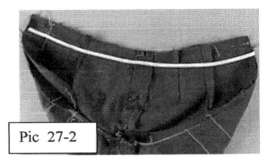

Pic 27-2

Tip: *To easily remark the new waist seam place a narrow tape on the new seam, baste stitch along it for a guideline when re-applying the waistband (pic 27-2). When one side is marked, repeat the process and copy the seam line on the other side.*

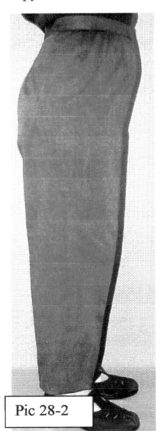

Pic 28-2

Re-evaluation after the second pin fitting

Compare picture 26-2 and picture 28-2. The front is looking much better on the profile. Linda likes her clothing loose so I will not remove any more ease in the high hip area.

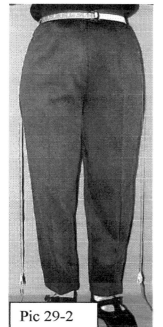

Pic 29-2

Pants with the plumb line belt in place for a final check on the hang of creases and side seams with the hem rolled up so the leg can hang properly (29-2).

Linda is taking a step forward (pic 30-2) and backward (pic 31-2) to check the fit. She sat down in the pants and reports that they are very comfortable.

She also has room to tuck her top into the pants.

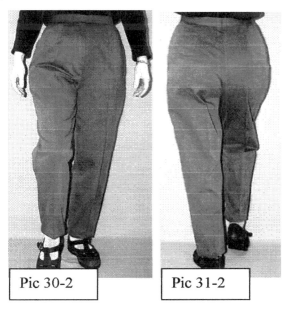

Pic 30-2

Pic 31-2

Comfort and good looks are both important not just when standing still but also when sitting and walking.

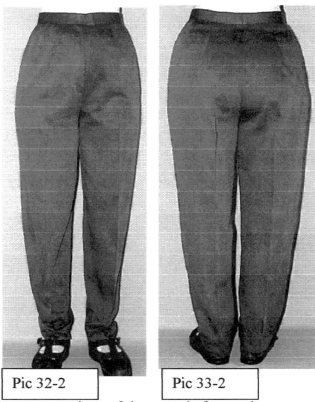

Pic 32-2

Pic 33-2

For a comparison of the pants before and after the pin fitting look at the front view picture 18-2 & 32-2 and the back view picture 20-2 & 33-2.

Leg length is individual. Some people like a break in the front leg, others want their pants to fall smoothly to the top of the shoe. Linda likes a break.

Linda can use this pant pattern for a fitted pant. She can adjust the pleated versions in Vogue 2946 exactly as this pattern was adjusted for a dressy slack. She can use it as a drafting tool and she can use it as a guide to adjust a new pattern. I recommend using the basic and the pleated views instead of adjusting a new pattern.

Example 3: Linda Basic Pant Pattern

Linda has never had a pair of pants, not even jeans that she considered comfortable. She has worn very loose fitting styles of pants. She wants a comfortable pair of pants and more styles than a slim leg. Vogue 2946 View E has a slim pant to use as a basic pattern, and other views that will give her the choice of making dressy slacks. Comparing her measurements to the Industry Standard Measurement Chart, we found that Linda is between a size 12 and 14 at the hip line in Vogue 2946. Her crotch depth was very close to the size 14 pattern and she likes her garments loose so we chose to use the size 14 pattern. We will take in the side seam to maintain a narrow leg and let out the front and back crotch to fit her front and back curves.

To facilitate adjustment, we copied the flat tissue measurements of the basic pattern in size 14 from the Industry Standard Chart to her pant measurement chart in the spaces provided.

Begin by checking the pattern in the sequence below before changing the pattern: The numbers used are from Linda's pant measurement chart that follows.

6. Crotch depth: Linda's crotch depth measures 11 inch; 1 inch ease was added for a total of 12 inches. The pattern measures 11 ¾ inches. No adjustment on the crotch depth is needed before the tissue fitting.

8. Waist to floor length: Linda's measurement is 39 1/8 inches. The pattern measures 40 ½ inches. Shorten the pattern 1-¼ inches at the hem.

9. Waistline adjustments: Linda measures ¼ longer at center back than at center front indicating that the center back seam at the waistline needs to be raised ¼ inch. Since the difference is small, use a 1 inch seam allowance at the waist line, and adjust the waistline when it is in fabric using the plumb line as your guide.

7. Crotch length: She measures 28 inches from the center back to the center front. The pattern measures 27 ¼ inches. Compare the back and front crotch lengths. Linda's back crotch is 15 inches; the pattern back crotch is 14 7/8 inches. Her front crotch is 13 inches; the pattern is 12 3/8 inches. Add 3/8 inch to the center back inseam and 3/8 to the center front inseam.

1a. Waistband length: The waistband length on the size 14 pattern is 29 inches. Linda needs a waistband of 28 inches. The waistband is one piece, cut it at the center back and add a seam line making sure each side measures 14 inches.

1. Waist seam: The waist seam of the slacks must measure 1 inch larger than the waistband. The pattern measures 29 ½ inches; Linda needs 29 inches. Adjust for the difference at the side seams and the center front and center back seams.

2. Hip width at 3 inches: The pattern measures 38 ½ inches; Linda measures 35 ½ without ease. She wants her pants comfortable with plenty of room to tuck in her tops. Adjust the waist seam and the 9 inch hip line and pin fit the hip at the 3 and 7 inch areas on the side seam.

3. Hip width at 7 inches: The pattern measures 41 ¾ inches; Linda measures 38 ¾ without ease. Adjust the waist seam and the 9 inch hip line and pin fit the hip at the 3 and 7 inch areas on the side seam.

4. Hip width at 9 inches: The pattern measures 42 inches; Linda measures 39 without ease. Allow 3 inches ease in the 9 inch hip line. Add at the center back and front crotch seams to accommodate her curves and take the side seam where she is not as curved as indicated by the measurements.

5. Thigh width: Linda has a slim thigh. The pattern will be adjusted for her hip and crotch; the thigh won't need any other adjustment.

The changes listed are reflected on her pattern tissue as shown in the full view (sk 22-2 & 23-2) and the close up views (sk 25-2 & 26-2.

Example 3 Linda's Basic Pant Pattern

Pant Measurement Chart

Personal Body Measurements: Name: ____Linda____Date: 01-04-00

Pattern _Vogue 2946____Pattern size: _14_____

Flat Pattern Measurement	**Waist& Hip Measurements**⊗ (Take with a plumb line belt) Take or copy 1 through 4 from the dress measurement chart.
1._29 3/4____	**1.**Waist_26 1/2___ snug , but relax & breathe easy add 1 ½ to 2 inches __28_____
	Waistline of pants pattern is Waist band measurement plus 1 inch ___29_____
1a _29_____	**1a**. Waistband length ___28_____ width____1 1/4_____
1b. _14 1/2___	**1b**. ½ of the waistband_____14_____
2. _38 1/2___	**2.** 3 inches from waist __35 1/2_ + 1-1 ¼ inches ease _36 3/4
3. __41 3/4__	**3.** 7 inches from waist _38 3/4___ + 1 3/4- 2 inches ease _40 1/2___
4. __42____	**4.** 9 from waist _39_____ + 2-3 inches ease _41_____
	4a. Hip at the largest _39_____ Distance from waistline __9_____inches
	4b. Tape just slips off hip line- shows minimum amount of ease in a close fitted slack_41____

Additional measurements for slacks
Take sitting on a flat surface.

5. __26 1/2__	**5.** Largest thigh __21_____ mark the leg then note the distance from the waist when standing _13_____
6. __11 3/4__	**6.** Crotch depth __11_____ from waist to the flat surface 1-2 inches ease __12_____

Take standing

7 ._27 1/2_	**7.** Crotch length from center front to center back ___28_____
7a _12 3/8____	**7a.** Front crotch length __13_____ Front curve_____9_____
7b._14 7/8__	**7b.** Back crotch length __ 15_____ Back Curve _____9 1/2___
8. __40 1/2	**8**. Waist to floor____39 1/8_____
	8a. Waist to knee ____24 1/4_____

9. Waistline Adjustments: Length from waist to floor

. Center back __39 1/4____ Left side __39 3/8

Center front ____39_____ Right side _39 3/8

Full view of adjusted front pattern

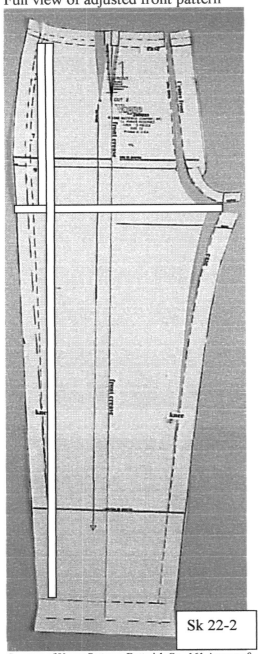

Sk 22-2

Courtesy of Vogue Patterns, Butterick Co., 161 Avenue of
the Americas, NY, NY 10013

Full view of adjusted back pattern

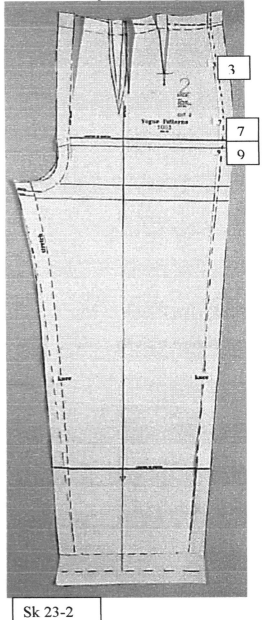

Sk 23-2

FRONT TISSUE:

The numbers are in the adjustment sequence

6. Crotch depth: Crotch depth was lowered ¼ at the side seam (sk22-2 & 25-2).

8. Waist to floor length: The pattern was shortened 1 ¼ inches at the hem line. The pattern is overlapped (sk 22-2 & 23-2).

9. Waistline adjustments: The center front was lowered ½ inch (sk 25-2).

7. Crotch length: The center front crotch curve was raised ½ inch and lengthened at the inseam 5/8 inch. The front crotch now measures 11 ¾ inches (sk 25-2).

1a. Waistband length: The waistband was shortened ½ inch to make the front and back waistbands 14 inches long (sk 24-2).

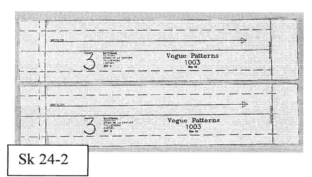

Sk 24-2

1. Waist seam: The front waist seam was taken in ½ inch at the side seam. The center front seam was increased 3/8 of an inch. The front dart was let out 1/8 inch at the waistline. The extra ¼ inch is eased onto the waistband with as much as possible eased between the dart and the center front. The dart was moved to correspond with the front crease line to fit Linda's front curve (sk 25-2).

2. Hip width at 3 inches: The side seam at the 3 inch line was taken in ½ inch.

3. Hip width at 7 inches: The side seam at the 7 inch line was taken in 3/8 inch (sk 25-2).

4. Hip width at 9 inches: The side seam at the 9 inch hip line was taken in 3/8 inch.

The hip adjustment was tapered into the pattern seam at the hem line (sk 25-2).

5. Thigh width: The front thigh was increased because of the addition to the front curve at the inseam (sk 25-2).

Close up of adjusted front pattern

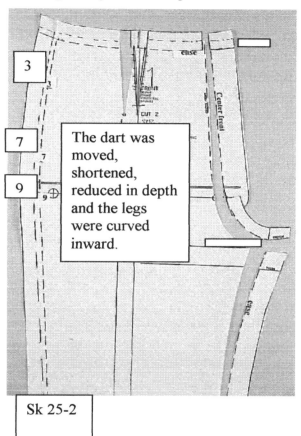

The dart was moved, shortened, reduced in depth and the legs were curved inward.

Sk 25-2

Courtesy of Vogue Patterns, Butterick Co., 161 Avenue of the Americas, NY, NY 10013

BACK TISSUE:

6. Crotch depth: Crotch depth was lowered ¼ by overlapping at the waist side seam marked with a small bar (sk 22 –2 & 26-2).

8. Waist to floor length: The pattern was shortened 1 ¼ inches at the hem line. (The pattern is overlapped) (sk 23–2).

9. Waistline adjustments:

7. Crotch length: The center back crotch curve was lowered 5/8 inch. The inseam was taken in 5/8 inch at the crotch and tapered to the knee. The back crotch now measures 14 inches (sk 26-2).

1a. Waistband length: The waistband was shortened ½ inch to make the back waistband 14 inches long (sk 24-2).

1. Waist seam: The back waist seam was taken in 3/8 inch at the side seam. The center back seam was increased 3/8 of an inch. The back derriere dart was increased 3 /16 of an inch on each leg at the waistline for a total of 3/8 inch. The dart was lengthened to 5 ½ inches and the legs curved out (convex) to remove excess width above the derriere. The dart was moved ½ inch to fit Linda's back curve (sk 26-2).

2. Hip width at 3 inches: The side seam at the 3 inch line was taken in 3/8 inch (sk 26-2)..

3. Hip width at 7 inches: The side seam at the 7 inch line was taken in 3/8 inch (sk 26-2)..

4. Hip width at 9 inches: The side seam at the 9 inch hip line was taken in 3/8 inch and tapered to the hem. The hip adjustment is tapered into the pattern seam at the hem line (sk 26-2)..

5. Thigh width: The back thigh was decreased because the back leg at the inseam was taken in. (sk 26-2).

Courtesy of Vogue Patterns, Butterick Co., 161 Avenue of the Americas, NY, NY 10013

Close up of adjusted back pattern

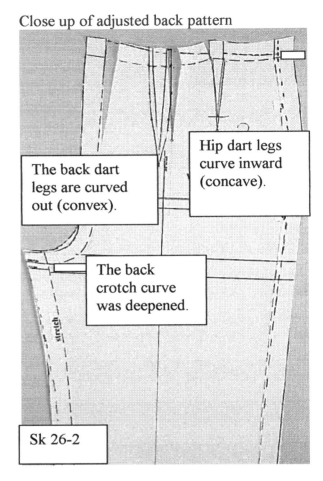

The back dart legs are curved out (convex).

Hip dart legs curve inward (concave).

The back crotch curve was deepened.

Sk 26-2

Final review of Linda's pattern changes after the pin fittings.
Linda's crotch length measurement is longer than her adjusted pattern measures and yet the pants look nice and are comfortable.
Explanation: The waistline is fitting on her hipbones instead of up at her true waistline. Her front inseam is longer than her back inseam. The back inseam was stretched with a steam iron before sewing it to the front inseam where the front was eased onto the shorter back from knee to the crotch. This technique helps the back under the derriere hang as smooth as possible.

All measurements are guidelines in adjusting a pattern. The real test is on the body. Is it comfortable? Are you happy with the way it looks? Linda's pattern passed those tests with flying colors.

Chapter 3

Fitting Tools and How to Use Them

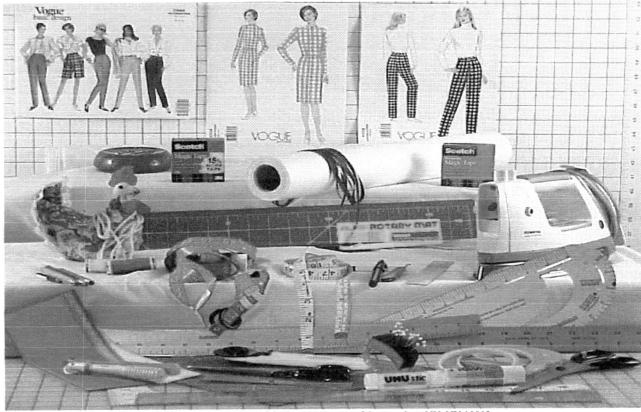

Courtesy of Vogue Patterns, Butterick Co., 161 Avenue of the Americas, NY, NY 10013

Patterns:
Vogue Pattern 1004 for your fitting dress in the correct size.

Vogue Patterns 1003 or 2946 View E for your pants in the correct size.
1003 has a slightly narrower leg, has only fitting ease and is strictly a fitting basic.
2946 View E has a narrow leg, wearing and design ease and has other views for fashion pants.

Pattern Altering Supplies:
Backing paper: Should be at least 20 inches wide. I use paper that is not slick from a medical supply store.

Tapes:
Masking tape or Fine line: Fine line tape is available in many narrow widths and can usually be found at automobile paint supply stores. Use either tape to mark and blend seam lines.

Scotch tape: Magic tape (green box) in either ¾ or ½ inch widths. Use to reinforce the pattern on the wrong side and to permanently tape small areas on the tissue pattern.

Removable tape: Use Scotch Magic Tape (blue box) to tape areas and seam lines on the tissue that may be changed. A seam can be marked on it and them moved after a tissue fitting.

Glue stick: Use to glue the pattern to the backing paper when you will not be moving that area. Glue is a better option than tape.

Removable glue stick: Can be purchased at an office supply store. It is the same glue that is on sticky note pads. Holds a tissue to the backing paper or another part of the pattern but allows it to be moved. Use this rather than either tape.

Pencils and Pens:

Pencils: Softest lead pencil to mark seam lines on the tissue.

Pen: Black medium tip felt pen to permanently mark new seam lines and darts.

Grease pencil: Eyebrow or grease pencil to mark the shoulder and armhole locations on the body.

Colored pencils: Red and green pencils to mark stitching lines on an asymmetrical pattern.

Measuring Devices:

Tape measure (fiberglass): The easiest to use are tape measures, which begin at 1 inch on opposite ends.

Plastic ruler: 2 inch by 18 inch transparent ruler with calibrations in sixteenths to the inch. (C-thru is a common brand)

Dritz French curve: Used to mark curved seam lines.

Hip Curve: Used to draw and blend the hip curve on skirts and the hip and leg curve on pants.

Ruler: A 6 inch metal ruler: Great for measuring small areas.

Yardstick: Preferably a metal yardstick for marking long seamlines and redrawing straight of grain lines.

Plumb line belt: A plumb line belt is used to take correct front and back width and armhole measurements, to establish the correct seam line in skirt and pants and to judge the hang of one piece garments as well as the walking room in buttoned garments. Weighted drapery cord: The cord is included in the plumb line belt kit and is used to establish a jewel neckline and fitted armhole. It can be used as a plumb line.

Cutting Devices:

Cutting mats: Large and small cutting mats make pattern alteration much faster than cutting the tissue entirely with scissors. I use a long narrow piece of a cutting mat to work between the tissue and the backing paper.

Rotary cutter: Rotary cutters are fast and accurate for cutting pattern tissues.

Paper scissors: Use scissors for trimming tissue and clipping small areas.

Fabric scissors: Use for cutting and sewing the fitting garments.

Sewing and marking supplies for making the fitting dress and pants:

Fabric: Weavers cloth or other firm woven fabric to make the fitting garments. I prefer a firmer fabric instead of muslin. Preshrink and straighten the grain.

Straight pins: Use pins for sewing the basic muslin and for pinning the tissue together for the tissue fitting.

Tracing paper and tracing wheel: Used to mark seams, darts and grain lines on the fitting garments.

Contrast thread: Use to mark all seams and cross grain lines and a different color thread for sewing the seams and for altering seams.

Narrow ribbon: Narrow ribbon is used to pin at the waist of the fashion patterns.

Seam ripper: To open seams at the pin fitting.

Hand needles: To hand stitch small areas or thread trace an occasional seam.

Mirror : Mirrors enable you to judge the pattern. A three-way mirror is the best but a full-length mirror and a hand held mirror would work fine.

Adjusting Darts

A dart is a shaped tuck that is wide at the seam line and narrows at the dart end. Darts are used to build shape into a flat piece of fabric. Darts must be shaped to fit your curves and must end slightly before the fullest part of the body they are shaping. Pin fit the tissue to ensure the fit, mark the darts accurately, stitched them carefully and press darts gently.

Straight darts

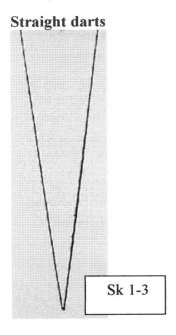

Sk 1-3

Darts give fullness and build shape into a garment where it is needed with straight dart legs (sk 1-3).

Lengthened dart

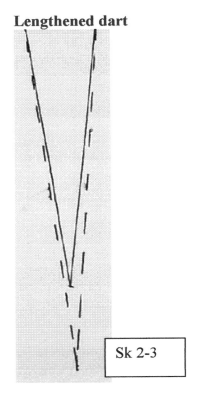

Sk 2-3

Concave darts

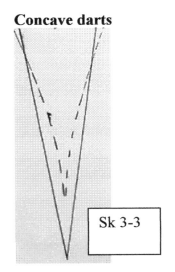

Sk 3-3

A straight dart can be changed to give more room when the legs are curved inward, a concave curve (sk 3-3). It can be left long (sk4-3) or shortened to fit the body curves. (sk 3-3.

Long concave dart

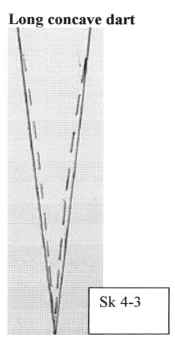

Sk 4-3

Use concave darts when you need shaping but more room than a straight dart allows (sk 4-3).

Convex dart

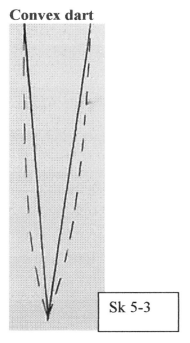

Sk 5-3

Darts can remove extra ease by making the dart legs curve outward, a convex curve (sk 5-3). A convex dart makes a garment fit move closely in areas where there needs to be shaping but a straight dart leg leaves too much fullness above the end of the dart. The most common areas for convex darts are under the bust line and above the derriere.

Check the position, the length and the shape of the darts when you pin fit the tissue. Change the shape and size of the darts if needed. Check the darts again when you pin fit the muslin fitting garments and do any other changes that are needed.

Marking and sewing darts
Mark the darts carefully with tracing paper and a tracing wheel on the fitting garments. Use other methods of marking darts on fashion fabric. Stitch the darts carefully staying on the marked lines. It is important on every dart shape to have a tapered point at the end of the dart. Refer to The Art Of Sewing Basics & Beyond for quality sewing techniques that are indispensable when making beautiful clothing.

Reference Material:
The Art Of Sewing Basics & Beyond
Author: Shirley L. Smith

Threads Magazine, issue 79
Darts Build Shape Into A Garment
Author: Shirley L. Smith

Marking and Sewing the Fitting Muslins

It is important to be very accurate when cutting, marking and sewing the basic fitting muslins.

Use a firm woven cloth, such as weavers cloth, or very good quality muslin that is straight of grain. Brushed denim or just denim with no stretch will work for a fitting pant that can be worn.

Press the pattern and the fabric.

Dress Basic

The fitting dress has a front opening that is pinned closed when the dress is being fitted.

One-inch seam lines have been allowed everywhere except at the center back seam line, the neckline and armhole of the bodice. Allow a one or two inch hem on the skirt.

If you do not have symmetrical sides but you have only tissue fit half a pattern, cut both sides of the garment on the largest side's cutting line. Mark the right hip and waist stitching lines with a red stitch. Mark the left hip and waist stitching lines with a green stitch. When you stitch the skirt front and back together and the skirt to the bodice use the correct stitching line on the left and right sides of the garment.

Do not trim seams or finish edges until the pin fitting.

- Cut the garment with scissors or rotary cutter, NOT pinking shears. Cut the fabric exactly as the tissue has been trimmed.

- Mark all seam lines and cross grain lines (front and back bodice bust line, front and back 9-inch hip line, sleeve cap, and bicep line), accurately with a tracing wheel using a ruler to keep the lines straight. Then machine baste with a contrast color so seam lines and cross

grain lines can be easily seen on both sides of the fabric

Option: Mark on both sides of the fabric with the tracing wheel and tracing paper. Test to make sure that the marks will withstand steaming when the seams are pressed.

- Stitch all the darts **stopping the stitching at the seam line and backstitch**.

- Stitch the skirt center front to within 7" of the waistline. Leave the bodice front open.

- Ease stitch (machine-baste) the entire sleeve cap on the seam line. Do a second row of stitching in the seam allowance. Pull the threads and gather the cap, then smooth the gathering until there are no puckers. Steam shrink the cap. Since weavers cloth or muslin are difficult to ease don't worry if you have some tiny puckers when the sleeve is basted in the armhole.

- Machine baste the entire garment with a different color thread than you used to mark the seams. Use a longer stitch than you would ordinarily use to construct a garment but short enough so it does not come apart while you are pin fitting. **Stop the stitching at the seam line and backstitch.**

- **Do not stitch across seam lines.** Stitch to the seam line and backstitch. Begin on the other side of the seam, leaving the seams floating.

- Lightly press all the seams open.

- Measure up the hem evenly as marked on the pattern and baste it in place.

You are now ready to pin fit the basic muslin.

Pant Basic

The fitting pant has a front opening that is pinned closed when fitting.

One-inch seam lines have been allowed everywhere except at the under crotch seam line.
Allow a two-inch hem on the pants.

If you are not symmetrical but you have only tissue fit half a pattern, cut both sides of the garment on the largest side cutting line. Mark the right hip and waist stitching lines with a red stitch. Mark the left hip and waist stitching lines with a green stitch. When you stitch the pants front and back together and the pants to the waistband use the correct stitching line on the left and right sides of the garment.

Do not trim seams or finish edges until the pin fitting.

- Cut the garment with scissors or rotary cutter, NOT pinking shears. Cut the fabric exactly as the tissue has been trimmed.

- Mark all seam lines and cross grain lines (front and back 9-inch hip line), accurately with a tracing wheel using a ruler to keep the lines straight. Then machine baste with a contrast color so seam lines and cross grain lines can be easily seen on both sides of the fabric

Option: Mark on both sides of the fabric with the tracing wheel and tracing paper. Test to be sure that the marks will withstand steaming when the seams are pressed.

- Press the front crease line before stitching the darts.

- Stitch all the darts stopping the stitching at the seam line and backstitch.

- Stitch the pants center front to within 7" of the waistline. Leave the center front open.

- Machine baste the entire garment with a different color thread than you used to mark the seams. Use a longer stitch than you would ordinarily use to construct a garment but short enough so it does not come apart while you are pin fitting. **Stop the stitching at the seam line and backstitch.**

- **Do not stitch across seam lines.** Stitch to the seam line and backstitch. Begin on the other side of the seam, leaving the seams floating.

- Lightly press all the seams open

- Measure up the hem evenly as marked on the pattern and baste it in place.

You are now ready to pin fit the basic slack muslin.

Transfer the Pin fitting Adjustments

All pin fitting is done on the right side of the garment. It must be transferred accurately to the wrong side of the garment. Although both sides of the garment will be pinned to ensure an accurate pin fitting mark only one side of the altered garment unless you are very different on left and right sides. Since it is very difficult to pin fit both sides exactly the same, choose the side that looks the best, mark the seam on that side transferring the marking to the other side. The new seam line must blend with the original seam line.

Pinned tuck

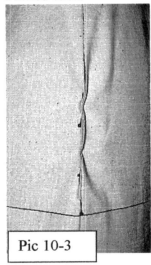

Pic 10-3

A seam pinned to remove some hip curve between the 3-inch and 7-inch area of the hip line (Pic 10-3). The seam is pinned the amount to remove.

Pinned flat most accurate

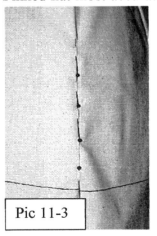

Pic 11-3

The seam is pinned flat to remove hip curve. Either way of pinning works. The flat method gives a very accurate idea of how the garment will look (Pic 11-3). Both sides of the skirt will be taken in. Use narrow

masking or fine line tape to give a new straight, blended seam line (Pic 12-3).

Marking the Muslin

Mark the two layers of fabric where they touch with pins or a thread trace. Mark the **turn** where the fabric is folded on the upper layer and the **touch** where the fold lies on the under layer (sk 12-3).

Thread trace

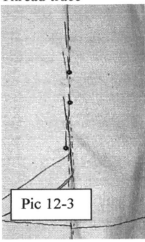

Pic 12-3

To mark the new seam with a thread trace, baste in the fold of the upper layer marking the **turn**.

Baste a line exactly where the fold lies on the under layer marking the **touch**.

Adjustment marked with pins

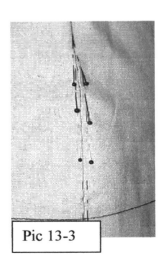

Pic 13-3

To mark with pins, put pins in at intervals in the fold of the fabric and where the fold touches the under layer (Pic 13-3). Go to the wrong side of the fabric and mark the location of the pin with a chalk or marking pencil.

Then mark the same adjustment on the other side of the garment.

Marking the Tissue
It is very important to mark the pin fitting changes on the tissue. The corrected tissue is invaluable as a guide when you are adjusting commercial fashion patterns. Place removable Magic Tape on the tissue where the changes will be marked. The tape strengthens the area and if the seam has to be changed the tape can easily be removed.

Transfer pin fitting from muslin to tissue with pins

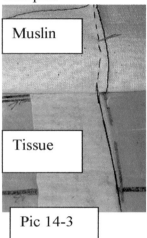

Muslin

Tissue

Pic 14-3

To mark the tissue, place the muslin back on the tissue, carefully lining up edges and any guideline marks such as the hip line on both the muslin and tissue. Stick pins through the muslin (pic 14-3) into the tissue along the corrected seam line and mark.

Muslin hip line marked with a machine baste

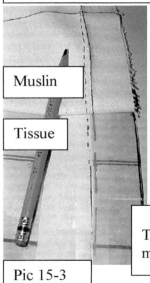

Muslin

Tissue

Pic 15-3

Alternatively, as in picture 15-3 lift the muslin in small sections and mark with a pencil line.

Tissue hip line marked on the pattern

Mark the seam with fine line tape

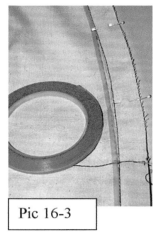

Pic 16-3

Stitch the Corrected Muslin
Stitch the pin fit seam on the new seam line. Use 1/8 inch or 1/4-inch fine line tape (Refer to Chapter 2 Fitting Tools) or masking tape to mark the seam line and to blend it with the original seam line (sk 16-3).

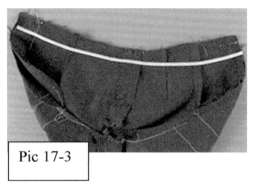

Pic 17-3

Fine line tape is a good way to judge the curve of a seam that varies in depth. When you are pleased with the curve of the seam, either machine or hand baste along the edge of the tape to mark the seam.

It is very important to transfer the corrections from your fitted muslin to your basic tissue.

The basic tissue is your guide when adjusting fashion patterns in Part 11 of the workbook.

Store your tissue carefully (a paper roll works well), use it as a reference when adjusting all other fashion patterns.

PART 11

APPLYING CUSTOM FITTING

Shirley in her stripped and checked silk noil pants and vest and
cotton t-shirt made from a Sewing Workshop pattern
Vogue 2522
Designer Original Issey Miyake

CHAPTER 4

Choosing & Evaluating Fashion Patterns

This workbook does not attempt to cover the most flattering styles for every figure type. Be realistic when paging through the pattern book looking for that new sewing project. If

you wear larger than a 'B' cup bra, choosing styles with some gathers or pleats at the front shoulder, or a princess style guarantees good results without many changes. If you choose a pattern with no bust shaping, you must add some bust shaping or you will have a poorly fitting garment.

Your measurements tell you whether you are a Triangle, inverted triangle, rectangle or hourglass figure type.

Triangle:

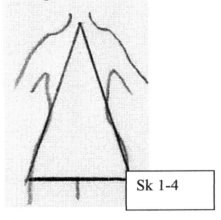

Sk 1-4

If your measurements are larger in the hip than the bust line and you have narrow shoulders you are a triangle figure type.

Inverted Triangle:

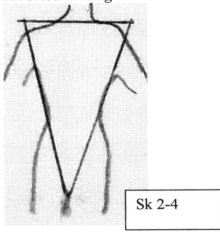

Sk 2-4

Broad shoulders, hips that are smaller than the bust, equal an inverted triangle figure type.

Rectangle

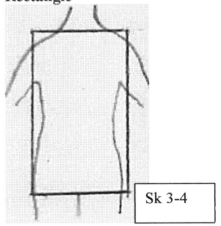

Sk 3-4

Hips and bust that are about the same measurement with little difference at the waist is a rectangle figure type.

Hourglass:

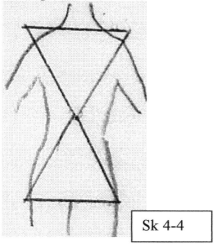

Sk 4-4

Bust and hips that measure about the same, with a small waist is an hourglass figure type.

 Some patterns have the figure type symbols on the pattern.

After having your measurements taken and seeing the alterations to your basic pattern you know where your figure varied from the industry standard. You know what features you want to emphasize and those you wish to minimize. Choosing styles that are flattering to your figure type simplifies pattern adjustment.

Study the pattern description; sometimes it is a photograph, which is helpful, sometimes an artist sketch of the garment. There are always line drawings of the front and back view that often give a better indication of the garment than the picture. Always read the description of the garment, if it is available, and study the line drawing on the back of the pattern envelope. The description tells you the silhouette of the garment, close fitted, fitted, semi-fitted, loose fitted, or very loose fitted and describes the fit of the shoulders, forward, dropped or extended and other important details that help you make an informed decision before buying the pattern. The silhouette is the clue to the amount of ease in the pattern.

Vogue patterns have a misses ease allowance chart for close-fitted, fitted, semi-fitted, loose-fitted and very loose fitted silhouettes (page 106). The chart is also in their pattern book so when you are shopping you have an idea of the ease in their fashion patterns.

As you can see on the Misses Ease Allowance Chart, the design ease varies greatly in some silhouettes. The pattern envelope suggests the best weight and type of fabric to use and tells you if you must use a nap layout. There are also lengths of garments and skirt and pant leg width measurements to guide your buying decision.

Design and Wearing Ease
Wearing ease: The ease that was added to your measurements when your basic dress was adjusted is enough room to move and breathe comfortably. Usually the ease added is: Full bust 2-3 inches, Waist 1-1½ inches, Hip 2 inches.

Design ease: The ease the designer put into the fashion pattern to give it style.

To determine the ease in commercial fashion patterns follow the three steps below:

One: Note the measurements for your size on the measurement chart at the bust, waist and 9 inch hip line. This chart is on the flap of every pattern envelope.

Two: Note the flat tissue measurement of your pattern in the bust, waist, and 9 inch hip line. Most patterns have this symbol '⊕' at the bust and hip line on the tissue and give the flat tissue measurement for each size included in the pattern. They do not always give the flat waist measurement.

Three: Flat tissue measurement of your pattern **minus** pattern envelope measurement in your size **equals the total** wearing and design ease. To determine just the design ease **subtract y**our wearing ease **from the total ease.** (Refer to page with examples).

After you have determined the amount of design ease in the garment you must decide if you will you be comfortable in that amount of design ease. Design ease depends on your taste, your build and height. It is very individual!
Most of you don't really know how much design ease you enjoy wearing. However, you have favorite clothing in your closet. Measure some favorite garments to determine how much total ease you enjoy wearing.

Measure a blouse worn under suits, a shirt blouse, your favorite fitted jacket, a loose jacket, a straight skirt, and a flared skirt. To measure, button the garment, place it on a flat surface and measure from side to side at the armhole and the hip line. Measure skirt and jacket lengths. Measure the waistline, hipline, and the bottom width of your favorite skirt and pants.

Make notes of the garment you are measuring, your weight and the date you did this research.

To determine the total ease in your favorite garments subtract your measurements without wearing ease (from your Dress Measurement Chart) from the measurement of your favorite garment.
The difference in your body measurements without ease and your garments is the wearing and design ease of the garments in your closet.

Subtracting the wearing ease that was added to your measurements (from your Dress Measurement Chart) tells you the amount of design ease in your favorite garments. Knowing the ease of comfortable garments will give you guidelines to use when adjusting patterns.

A word of caution, if you use the same amount of design ease in every garment you may destroy the very look you admired in the pattern book. Consider the look the designer has created when you adjust the design ease in a new pattern.[*]

Misses Ease Allowance Chart

Silhouette	dresses, blouses, skirts, tops, vests	jackets lined or not	coats lined or not
close fitting	0-2 7/8 inches	not applicable	not applicable
fitted	3-4 inches	3 ¾ - 4 ¼ inches	5 ¼ -6 ¾ inches
semi-fitted	4 1/8 -5 inches	4 3/8 - 5 ¾ inches	6 7/8 - 8 inches
loose fitting	5 1/8 - 8 inches	5 7/8 - 10 inches	8 1/8 - 12 inches
very loose fitting	over 8 inches	over 10 inches	over 12 inches

Measurement Chart from the flap of the Pattern Envelope

Size	6	8	10	12	14	16	18	20	22	24
Bust							30 ½	31 ½	32 ½	34
	36	38	40	42	44	46				
Chest	28 ½	29 ½	30 ½	32	34	36	38	40	42	44
Waist	23	24	25	26 ½	28	30	32	34	37	39
Hip	32 ½	33 ½	34 ½	36	38	40	42	44	46	48
Back Waist	15 ½	15 ¾	16	16 ¼	16 ½	16 ¾	17	17 ¼	17 3/8	17 ½

[*] Courtesy of Vogue Patterns, Butterick Co., 161 Avenue of the Americas, NY, NY 10013

Adjusting Fashion Patterns

Using the knowledge, you have gained about how your body differs from the industry standard and about wearing and design ease is the most efficient and accurate way to adjust commercial fashion patterns. Lay the basic on your fashion pattern only to locate a specific area such as the end of the shoulder, but **don't try to adjust your fashion patterns by laying the basic on the new pattern.**
For a garment to fit you must have wearing ease. For the garment to look like the picture on the pattern envelope you must have design ease. But how much? You can control the amount of design ease.

To begin, check the amount of ease by subtracting the pattern envelope measurements from the flat tissue measurements. As you can see in the following examples of Vogue and Butterick patterns, the ease in patterns vary.
You know exactly how much wearing ease was added to your basic at the bust, waist and hip. Make sure the pattern fits those requirements and then add the design ease allowed by the pattern. This gives you the exact amount of ease the designer put in the pattern, which gives the garment the look you liked in the pattern book.

To control the ease, check the ease as shown in the examples on the following pages, and decided how much design ease you want in each new pattern. Remember the pattern was designed for a 5 foot 6 inch lady with an average figure.

Here are some guidelines:
- **Close fitting** styles require more adjustments than other silhouettes. Add at least as much wearing ease as was added to your basic fitting muslin. Exception is a knit fabric. A knit pattern usually has about two inches less ease than a pattern for woven fabric (example Vogue 9942). Your fitting dress was closely fitted. A fashion pattern usually has a little more total ease than your basic fitting dress.

- **Fitted:** Use your pattern as a guide and add at least as much wearing ease as was added to your basic fitting muslin. Add what you are comfortable wearing for design ease.

- **Semi-fitted silhouettes:** The design of the garment may or may not give you enough total ease. You must decide how much total ease will be comfortable.

- **Loose fitted:** This silhouette often has enough total design ease. Check the amount of ease over your wearing ease to make your design ease decision.

- **Very loose fitted:** You may want to eliminate some design ease in these patterns. If you are shorter than 5 foot 6 inches, it is usually safe to use one size smaller pattern than you normally wear.

Most commercial fashion patterns come in multiple sizes and the seam lines are unmarked. Multiple sizes are helpful if you are a combination size. With a little experience adjusting patterns, you can taper from one size to another in the areas that fit your body. To begin it will be easiest to use your correct size, the size of your basic dress, and add as you did on your basic dress.

Examples of the various silhouettes:
Close-fitting

9942 Very Easy Vogue: Close fitting, straight dress below med-knee or tunic has back zipper and below elbow or long sleeves. Close-fitting, tapered skirt, above ankle, has elastic waist and back slit. All have stitched hems. Moderate Stretch Knits only.

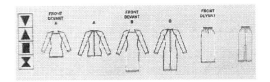

Size 12

Flat tissue measurement-Pattern envelope=Wearing & Design ease–Your Wearing ease=Design Ease

Bust	34 ¼"	34"	¼"	2"	minus 1 ¾"
Waist	30 ½"	26 1/2'"	4"	1 ½"	2 ½"
Hip	38"	36"	2"	2"	0"

Fitted

7152 Vogue: Fitted, partially interfaced line, below waist or hip length jacket has collar, shoulder pads, princess seams, fly button closing and long sleeves. Lined skirt, E & F are gored, slightly flared, above mid-knee, below mid-calf, or above ankle. Has waistband and back zipper. D: skirt is semi-fitted, straight, back slit.

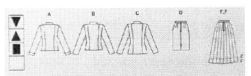

Size 12

Jacket

Flat tissue measurement-Pattern envelope=Wearing & Design ease-Your Wearing ease=Design Ease

Bust	37 ½"	34"	3 ½"	2"	1 ½"
Waist	33 ½"	26 ½"	7"	1 ½"	5 ½"
Hip	41 ½"	36"	5 ½"	2"	3 ½"
Skirt: Waist	27"	26 ½"	½"	1"	minus ½"
Hip	391/2" straight	36"	3 ½"	2"	1 ½"
	44 ½" flared	36"	8 ½"	2"	6 ½"

Courtesy of Vogue Patterns, Butterick Co., 161 Avenue of the Americas, NY, NY 10013

Semi-fitted

9389 Very Easy Very Vogue: Semi-fitted, lined, tapered dress, above mid knee, has shoulder pads, princess seams, front button trim, back zipper/slit and cap sleeves.

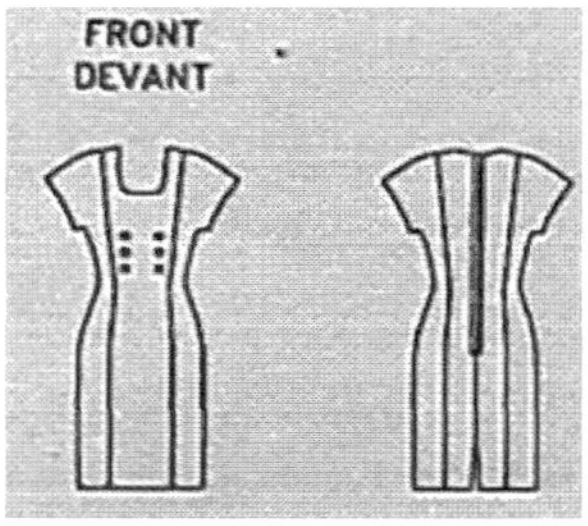

Tested pattern: The jacket is loose-fitted. A princess style dress is a good design for adjusting figures different from the industry standard. A shoulder princess (fitted seam line which that extends to the shoulder instead of the side seam) gives long vertical lines.

Size 12

Flat tissue measurement-Pattern envelope=Wearing & Design ease-Your Wearing ease=Design Ease

	Flat tissue measurement	Pattern envelope	Wearing & Design ease	Your Wearing ease	Design Ease
Bust	38 ¼"	34"	4 ¾"	2"	2 ¼"
Waist	30"	26 ½"	3 ½"	1"	2 ½"
Hip	39 ½"	36"	31/2"		
	2"	1 ½"			

Semi-fitted

4187 Butterick: Semi-fitted top has collar, shoulder pads, princess seams, back belt and long sleeves with pleats, plackets and button cuffs. Slightly flared, bias skirt, above ankle has elastic waistband. Straight-legged pants have elastic waist.

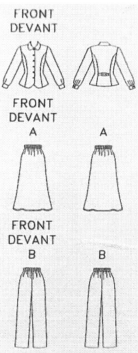

Tested Pattern: Princess seams are great for fitting figures different from the industry standard. This princess is the traditional princess as opposed to a shoulder princess. Both princess styles are great for larger than a B cup figures. They shape the bust line and have more seams for easier alterations.

Size 12

Flat tissue measurement-Pattern envelope=Wearing & Design ease-Your Wearing ease=Design Ease

		Flat tissue measurement	Pattern envelope	Wearing & Design ease	Your Wearing ease	Design Ease
Jacket--	Bust	38 ¾"	34"	4 ¾"	2"	2 ¼"
	Waist	33 ½"	26 ½"	7"	1"	6"
	Hip	42 ½"	36"	31/2"	2"	1 ½"
Skirt	Hip	46"	36"	10"	2"	8"
Pants	`Hip	43 ¼"	36"	7 ½"	2"	5 ½"

Courtesy of Vogue Patterns, Butterick Co., 161 Avenue of the Americas, NY, NY 10013

Loose-fitted

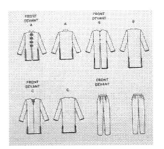

8867 Vogue Easy Options: Loose-fitting dress (semi-fitted through hips), above mid-knee or tunic has shoulder pads, side slits and long sleeves. Narrow hem.

Tested Pattern
A great pattern but it is without bust shaping. If you have larger than a B cup, add a bust dart to allow the pattern to hang plumb over the bust line.

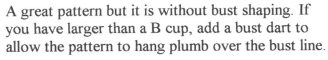

Size 12

Flat tissue measurement-Pattern envelope=Wearing & Design ease–Your Wearing ease=Design Ease

Bust	41 ½"	34"	7 ½"	2"	4 1/2
Waist	40"	26 ½"	13 ½"	1"	12 ½"
Hip	39 ¾"	36"	3 ¾"	2"	1 ¾

Loose-fitted

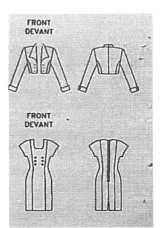

9389 Very Easy Very Vogue: Loose-fitting, lined, above waist jacket has contrast front extending into back collar, shoulder pads, side panels, no side seams and long sleeves with contrast cuffs.

Tested Pattern   The dress is Semi fitted.
This jacket has princess seams and a large dart at the side seam.
Suggestion: Add buttons on the jacket as trim.
Sew flat buttons on the dress as well to simplify buttoning the jacket onto the dress
Size 12

Flat tissue measurement-Pattern envelope=Wearing & Design ease-Your Wearing ease=Design Ease

Bust	40 ½"	34"	6 ½"	2"	4 ½"

Waist and Hip: No measurement for the jacket

Courtesy of Vogue Patterns, Butterick Co., 161 Avenue of the Americas, NY, NY 10013

Very Loose-fitted

4639 Butterick: Very loose-fitting, unlined, below hip jacket has collar variation, shoulder pads, pockets and long sleeves. View B & D are 2 inches longer than A & C.

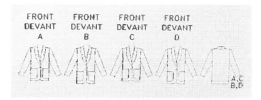

Size 12

Flat tissue measurement-Pattern envelope=Wearing & Design ease-Your Wearing ease=Design Ease

Bust	42"	34"	8"	2"	4"
Waist	42"	26 ½"	15 ½"	1"	14 ½"
Hip	42 ½"	36"	6 ½"	2"	4 ½"

Courtesy of Vogue Patterns, Butterick Co., 161 Avenue of the Americas, NY, NY 10013

Prepare the pattern:

- Trim and press the pattern to the correct size. (Trimming with a rotary cutter is fast and accurate).
- Mark 5/8" seam lines on the pattern pieces you will use for the tissue fitting. Usually these will be the bodice front and back, the sleeve, and the skirt front and back.
- Back the pattern with medical supply paper, gluing (with a glue stick or removable glue stick) small areas in the center of the pattern. Do not glue anywhere close to a seam that will be altered.

Design ease decision:

Determine how much ease is in the pattern, as was done in the examples above.
Write down the bust, waist and hip measurements for your size from the pattern envelope.
Check the flat tissue measurement.
Subtract the pattern envelope measurement from the flat tissue measurement. (Many patterns have the flat tissue measurement on the front pattern pieces. If not, measure the tissue from seam to seam at the bust waist and 9 inch hipline. (Do not include the seam allowances.) That gives you the wearing and design ease. Subtract your wearing ease to get the design ease that is allowed in the pattern. Then make your design ease decision.

Adjust the fashion pattern:
Follow the sequence that was used on your basic as is listed below.

- **Bodice Length:** Adjust as your basic was adjusted.

- **Bustline:** If you did a bust cup adjustment, you may or may not have enough ease in the bust area. Check the ease allowance in the bust area. There may be adequate ease without adjustment. If you must add to the bust and have a princess seam line, do the bust cup adjustment at the princess seam line and full bust adjustment at the side seams. If the princess pattern pieces have multiple size grading, add equally to seams with size grading. .

- **Front shoulder width:** Make sure it is at least as wide as your basic.

- **Shoulders: Always do any adjustments to your fashion pattern that were done to your basic fitting muslin at the shoulders. Since most garments hang from the shoulders, the fitting in the shoulders is most crucial.**

- **Back:** Adjustments to the upper back and the back width must always be checked and must be at least as wide as the basic.

- **Armhole:** Armhole adjustments vary with the sleeve style. If the garment is very loose fitting, the armhole is usually quite low or deep. Check the depth of the armhole of the new pattern and compare it to the depth of your basic. If the garment is close-fitted, the armhole must be high or you cannot move. You may want to raise the armhole. You can always lower it but you can raise it only 3/8 of an inch if you have not cut it high enough. Any changes to the armhole must have corresponding changes to the sleeve.

- **Neckline:** If you change the neckline of a pattern, you must change any facing or collar that attaches to the neckline. If the collar pattern is curved, adjust it in the same area as the neckline.

Sleeves: Measure the sleeve width at the armhole and adjust in the same manner your basic was adjusted. Gathered sleeves must be 1-1 ½ inches longer than the basic sleeve. Measure the sleeve plus the cuff. If sleeves have only one adjustment line for lengthening, add to the bottom of the sleeve.

Add a cross grain line in the cap area of the sleeve.
Raising the cap of the sleeve, the under arm seam of the sleeve and the bodice is a safety measure. If the cap or the underarm is too high, the excess can be cut off.

Waistline: Always do any adjustments to your fashion pattern that were done to your basic fitting muslin at the waist seam line.
Adjust the front and back seam of skirts and slacks if you have a prominent derriere or tummy. A high hip adjustment requires changes to the waist and hip. Other adjustments depend on the style of the garment.

- **Hipline:** Check the ease allowance in the hip area. If there is sufficient design ease in the garment, you may not need to add to the seams.

- **Length:** Check the length of the garment.

Skirts and Slacks
Waistbands:
The length of the waistband should always be checked and adjusted. Add a minimum of 1 inch to your waist measure for the waistband. If your waist becomes larger during the day, measure yourself in the evening. Make slack waistbands ½ to 1 inch larger than skirt waistbands.
Waist seam:
The waist seam of the skirt or slacks should be one inch larger than the waistband to allow ease for the waist indent and the hip curve. To adjust for the extra ease, make the darts smaller or add to the side seams.

After your pattern is adjusted, pin it together as you did the basic fitting muslin and pin fit the fashion pattern.

Tissue Fitting Fashion Patterns

Tissue fitting shows how the fashion pattern fits and how the garment will hang. You have adjusted your pattern using your basic and you knowledge of ease as your guide and now you will tissue fit the pattern to check those adjustments before cutting into your fabric.

Prepare the pattern:

Linda's fashion pattern

Of course, tissue fitting is easiest with help but if you put a narrow ribbon at the waistline of the pattern and some scotch the neckline front and back you can tissue fit your new pattern without the help a sewing friend (pic 1-4).

Pin or tape the tissue together as you did the basic pattern in Chapter 1 (pic 25-1 & 26-1). Some patterns, such as Neu Mode (no seam allowed) can be taped together with removable (blue label) Scotch Tape.

Pin the bodice front and back together at the sides and shoulders.

Pin a skirt onto the bodice.

Pin the sleeve together.

Pin any cuff onto the sleeve.

Pin the hemlines to the desired length.

Pin a seam tape or ribbon long enough to go around your waist and tie together to hold the pattern at your waistline. On a close fitting garment, put the tape on the outside. On a loose fitting garment pin the ribbon to the inside just enough to hold it at the waistline. On a garment with an unfitted waistline put the plumb line belt on underneath the tissue to

check the waistline (marked on the pattern) and the perpendicular hang of the center front and the center back.

If the pattern calls for a shoulder pad, pin the pad in place on the tissue.

Prepare yourself: Always wear the underclothing and shoes about the height that you will wear with the garment.

Tissue fit:

Slip the tissue on your body. Tie the ribbon around your waist. Pin the tissue to your clothing at the bust line front and back. Scotch tape will hold the pattern to your bare body. Slip the sleeve on and pin it to the bodice at match points in the front armhole. Match the big dot on the sleeve to the shoulder seam. If you have a helper, she can pin the back.

Evaluate your pattern: Evaluate your pattern paying close attention to the lengths of the pattern. The widths of a pattern are easy to adjust; the length and hang of the garment are more difficult.

Follow the sequence that was used on you basic pattern.

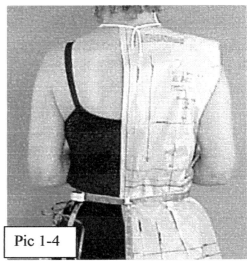

Pic 1-4

Courtesy of Vogue Patterns, Butterick Co., 161 Avenue of the Americas, NY, NY 10013

Bodice length: The ribbon at the waist of the tissue defines the waistline (sk 1-4, 2-4 & 3-

4). If there is blousing in the pattern make sure you are happy with the amount the pattern has allowed. You should be able to shrug your shoulder without straining the tissue for a comfortable bodice length.

Bust line: Is the bust line symbol $\oplus$ at your bust line? Bust darts should point to the bust and end before the fullest part of the bust. The pattern should come to the center front and the center back. If the pattern bust shaping is not at your bust line, it needs adjusting and should be at your bust line (pic 2-4).

Shoulders: The shoulder seam usually lies at the top of the shoulder. The shoulder seam ends at the hinge of the shoulder (pic 2-4). Shoulders often must be adjusted for a forward shoulder, (add to the back length at the shoulder) or square shoulders (add to both the back and front length at the shoulder).

Back Pattern: Check the back width of the pattern in the armhole. Make sure the shaping for the back is adjusted to your specifications.

Armhole: The depth of the armhole of a new tissue depends on the design ease. How deep is the armhole of your pattern? Check it against your basic by measuring the armhole of your new pattern and comparing it to the basic. If a garment is close fitted the armhole must be high, the looser the garment the lower or deeper the armhole can be. The armhole can always be raised at the tissue fitting and lowered at the pin fitting if it is too high. The armhole seam line should lie where the arm attaches to the body in the front and back (pic 3-4). If it is narrow in the back when you move your arms forward, straightening the back armhole curve will give more width.

Linda's fashion pattern

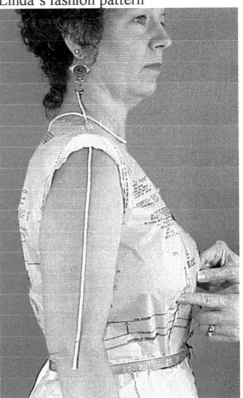

The shoulder has been moved forward, the bust line lowered to correspond with her basic pattern. Her fashion pattern calls for shoulder pads, a pad is pinned in place before the sleeve is pinned onto the bodice (pic 2-4).

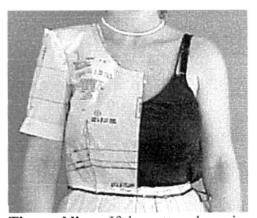

The neckline: If the pattern has a jewel neckline a weighted string around the neck helps establish a flattering and comfortable jewel neckline. Sometimes a neckline is too high in the front and too low in the back.

Courtesy of Vogue Patterns, Butterick Co., 161 Avenue of the Americas, NY, NY 10013

Sleeve: Sleeve should fit comfortably around the arm (pic 3-4). If the sleeve is long, check to make sure any elbow shaping is at your elbow when your arm is bent. Check the length of the sleeve by dropping your arm and extending your hand out; the pattern should touch your hand just below the wrist bone. If the sleeve is gathered or tucked with a cuff, it must be 1 ½ inches longer than your basic sleeve. Measure the fashion pattern sleeve with the cuff pinned in place.

Cuff: Check the cuff length. It should be 2 inches longer than your wrist for a close fitted buttoned cuff. If it is to be buttoned when the hand slips through the sleeve, the cuff pattern should be the hand measurement plus two inches.

Waist seam (bodice):
The ribbon at the waist will define the waistline (pic 5-4). Is the waistline of the garment at your waist? You can tell immediately if it is too short. Lifting your shoulders without straining the tissue will allow a comfortable amount of blousing in a bodice. If extra blousing is part of the design in the bodice be sure it is adequate.

Skirt: The darts on the front and back of the skirt should end at the fullest part of the body. The pattern should come to your center front and back. If it doesn't, let out the side seams.

The bodice back and the skirt darts that were altered to correspond with her basic are fitting nicely (pic 4-4 & 6-4).

Are the front and back seam lines hanging perpendicular or plumb? Check them with the plumb line. If the front of your pattern is not hanging plumb you may need to add more bust shaping than the pattern has included. If the back is not hanging plumb, you may need to take a tuck at the waistline.

Length: Check the length of a jacket or skirt and adjust the length for your body.

Linda's dress with the back plumb line

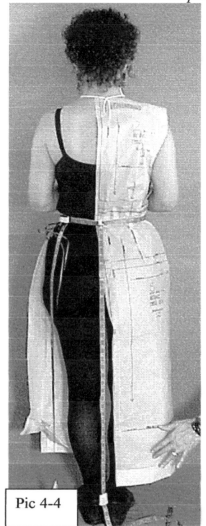

Pic 4-4

Linda's dress is not hanging plumb at center back. The skirt will be shortened at the center back waistline (pic 4-4).

Courtesy of Vogue Patterns, Butterick Co., 161 Avenue of the Americas, NY, NY 10013

Linda's dress with the center back seam hanging plumb

Pick 5-4

The sleeve has been added and checked. The dress has been shortened. Linda is happy with the way her tissue is fitting (pic 6-4).

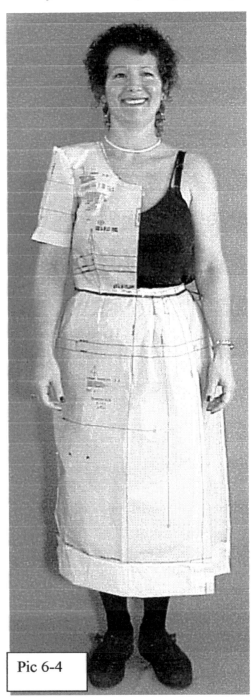

Pic 6-4

Notice the tuck pinned in the skirt just below the waistline marked with a bar (pic 5-4). The center back seam will be lowered during construction.

Make the needed corrections. Try the tissue back on and make sure you are happy with the pattern. If you are not completely satisfied, make a trial garment.

I make many garments without making a trial garment, however, when I have done several adjustments, especially lengthwise adjustments, I make a trial garment. It is especially important to make a trial garment when using expensive fabric.

The pattern will be unpinned and pressed before her garment is cut.

ourtesy of Vogue Patterns, Butterick Co., 161 Avenue of the Americas, NY, NY 10013

Pin Fitting Fashion Garments

Pin fitting is fine-tuning the fit as you sew. Do one alteration at a time as one alteration may affect or correct another problem. Pin fitting customizes the fit and makes your clothing comfortable. As soon as you get the major pieces of the garment together, try them on and check the fit.

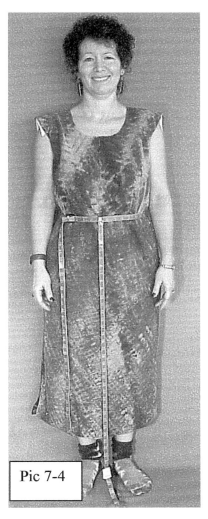

Pic 7-4

Never try the garment on wrong side out. Wear the correct undergarments. Don't over fit; too close a fit will accent a figure irregularity. Your garment should allow you to move comfortably (pic 7-4 & 11-4). **Pin fit only one side of the garment.** Then mark and adjust the other side in the same manner. If you make any changes at the pin fitting,

transfer the changes to the other side of the garment and back onto the tissue if you want to use the pattern again. Refer to Transferring Pin fitting Adjustments in Chapter 3.

Exception: If you are very different on the left and right side of your body you will need to pin fit each side.

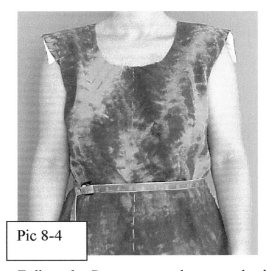

Pic 8-4

Follow the Sequence used on your basic and check the following:

Bodice length: Shrug your shoulders. Your bodice should not pull off the waistline.

Bodice front and Bust line: The garment should fit nicely in the bust line and any bust shaping should be at your bust tip and follow the contour of your bust line (pic 8-4). To check for the ease in the front width, straighten the shoulders and move the arms backward.

Shoulders: Bodices hang from the shoulders so the shoulder seam must lie on the top of your shoulder (pic 9-4). Often the fit can be improved by curving the shoulder seam to fit the contour of your shoulder.

Bodice Back: To check the ease and reach room in the back width after the sleeve is pinned or basted in place move the arms

117

forward and cross them. You should have adequate room. If needed let out the armhole seam on both the bodice and the sleeve cap in the back width.

Pic 9-4

Armhole: The armhole varies with the style of the sleeve. The most important consideration is comfort followed by appearance.

Neckline: The neckline should be comfortable and flattering.

Sleeve: Check the sleeve width, the length, and the hang of sleeve and fit of the cap area (10-4) . If the sleeve is a drop sleeve, raglan,

or a kimono sleeve the sleeve is loose and is usually not a problem. If the sleeve is a set-in-style, it should be pinned in the garment before permanently sewing. The sleeve cap cross grain line should always be marked with a thread trace. Pin the sleeve at the shoulder so the cross grain line is parallel to the floor. Pin the sleeve into the front and back armhole so the seam line appears straight and follows the body contour (Pic 10-4).

Pic 10-4

Waist seam of skirt: The lengthwise grain and seams of the skirt should hang straight or plumb (pic 10-4). (Use the Plumb line.) Seams that are not hanging straight indicate a need for re-checking the fit at the waistline (pic 9-4). Remove the skirt from the bodice, put the plumb line belt over the waist seam of the skirt. Adjust the skirt seam line up or down under the belt until the seams are hanging plumb with the plumb lines of the belt. Mark the bottom of the belt to establish a new waistline. Reattach the bodice. Occasionally if you have uneven hips the bodice seam line must be marked as well as the skirt.

Linda's dress needs to have the back waist seam lowered a slight amount to allow the side seam to hand plumb (pic 9-4). The bodice is fitting nicely. The dress is designed to skim the body and when the front drape is added after the pin fitting it gives a slimming line.

Hipline: Check the dart shaping and fit at the side seams. The darts should end just above your fullest point and they should be curved to fit your body.

Length: The final pin fitting is marking the hem.

Pic 11-4

When you finish your garment and try it on for the final inspection, it should meet all the requirements listed below of a good fit.

1. There should not be any stress on seams.

2. No wrinkles or excess fabric in unwanted places when standing still.

3. Lengthwise grain at center front and back should fall in the middle of the figure.

4. Crosswise grains should be parallel to the floor.

5. Shoulder seams should lie flat across the top of the shoulder and extend from the base of the neck to the shoulder hinge.

6. Side seams should hang straight and fall midway between front and back.

7. Lengthwise grain on the sleeve should be perpendicular to the floor above the elbow. The crosswise grain should be parallel to the floor.

You should be able to walk, sit, bend and reach comfortably in the garment.

When garments meet all those requirements, you will look and feel wonderful in your clothes.

Linda's dress fabric is her own hand dyed silk noil. The dress is lined with china silk except for the sleeves.

Her goal when she adjusted her basic pattern was to make clothing from her hand dyed fabric.

My goal in writing this book is to help you have as much success achieving a great fit as I have enjoyed. The clothing you see pictured throughout the book was constructed by students in the Sewing Arts Studio workshop classes. I have included a few garments that I especially enjoyed making and wearing.

Shirley Smith

Index

SHIRLEY SMITH is a teacher, clothing designer and expert in the field of garment construction. She has special expertise in fitting basic patterns and fashion patterns, both commercial and of custom design.

She studied under the direction of Elizabeth Nash, a master tailor from Vienna, Austria, and has been a student of New York designer Charles Kliebacher. From her sewing studio, founded in Denver in 1975, she authored and published her sewing text *The Art Of Sewing®: Basics & Beyond* which was adopted by colleges and universities across the country. She has authored *The Art Of Sewing® A Custom Fit workbook* released in March 2000. She is a contributing author to *Threads Magazine,* and was one of *Threads* magazine's fitting experts at a Creative Sewing and Needlework festival in Toronto.

She has produced two videos and designed a line of wearable-flower patterns. In 1996 Shirley and her husband moved to White Salmon, Washington to be near her daughters and grandchildren. In April of 1997 she opened a spacious new Sewing Arts® studio in the beautiful Columbia Gorge where she teaches workshop sewing and fitting classes and week long sewing and fitting seminars.

PRODUCTIONS by Shirley Smith

BOOKS:
The Art Of Sewing ®: Basics & Beyond: The book to help you sew professional, quality apparel, no matter what your skill level. Spiral bound, 350 pages illustrated, using 900 photographs.

The Art Of Sewing® A Custom Fit: A workbook that takes you step by step through the fitting process, then shows how to use the knowledge to adjust fashion patterns for a custom fit wardrobe. Spiral bound, 120 pages illustrated using 240 photographs and sketches.

Dressmakers Plumb line Kit: A tool to help you take accurate measurements and help you fit your garments.

VIDEOS:
The Art Of Sewing® Welt Pockets & Bound Buttonholes. Information on when to use bound buttonholes, when and where welt pockets may be added to a garment, and demonstrations on the construction of five styles of welt pockets. Two hour video.

The Art Of Sewing® Collars. Two hours of information on the four basic styles of collars, and construction and attachment to the garment of each style collar.

PATTERNS
Flower Patterns: # 103 Ultrasuede® & Facille Rose
                             #104 Ruffled Flowers, Roses & Sprays
                             #105 Chrysanthemums & Fringed Flowers

Pincushion Patterns: #101 Pig Pincushion
                                    # 102 Hen/Rooster Pincushion

ORDERING INFORMATION: THE SEWING ARTS® Studio
                                               175 Palos Verdes
                                               White Salmon, WA 98672

phone (509) 493-4490   email: sewingarts@gorge.net
Visit the Web site: http: //www.gorge.net/sewing_arts